In the
Midst of
Winter

In the Midst of Winter

Selections from the Literature of Mourning

Edited by

Mary Jane Moffat

Random House/New York

Copyright © 1982 by Mary Jane Moffat

All rights reserved under International and Pan-American
Copyright Conventions. Published in the United States by
Random House, Inc., New York, and simultaneously in
Canada by Random House of Canada Limited, Toronto.

Library of Congress Cataloging in Publication Data
Main entry under title:
In the midst of winter.
    1. Death—Literary collections.   2. Bereavement—
Literary collections.   I. Moffat, Mary Jane, 1933–
PN6071.D415   808.8'0354   81-19169
ISBN 0-394-52116-1   AACR2

Manufactured in the United States of America
24689753
First Edition

Acknowledgments

So many people have suggested selections for this book that I won't attempt to name them all.

I wish to express my appreciation to Charlotte Painter for her sustaining friendship and literary advice, to Dorothea Nudelman for reading the manuscript, and to Peg Lyons for research help. Among the many friends who gave comfort during my own season of mourning, Charles and Lucy Martell and Marian Schuster deserve special acknowledgment.

I also thank Anne Freedgood, my editor, and Maxine Groffsky, my literary agent, for their faith and encouragement.

Grateful acknowledgment is made to the following for permission to reprint previously published materials:

Aleixandre, Vicente, author: "My Grandfather's Death," translated by Stephen Kessler, from *Selected Poems of Vicente Aleixandre*, edited by Lewis Hyde, Harper & Row, Publishers, Inc. First published in *The Iowa Review*, Volume 9, Number 1. Copyright © 1978 by the University of Iowa. Reprinted by permission of Stephen Kessler, translator.

Altizer, Nell, author: "The Widow Teaches Poetry Writing." Copyright © 1982 by Nell Altizer. Reprinted by permission of the author.

Atheneum Publishers, Inc.: Peter Everwine, "Counting," from *Keeping the Night*. Copyright © 1977 by Peter Everwine (New York: Atheneum, 1977). Reprinted with the permission of Atheneum Publishers. Donald Justice, "First Death," from *Selected Poems*. Copyright © 1979 by Donald Justice (New York: Atheneum, 1979). Reprinted with the permission of Atheneum Publishers. Anne Philipe, from *No Longer Than a Sigh*, translated by Cornelia Schaeffer. Copyright © 1964 by Rene Julliard, Paris (New York: Atheneum, 1964). First published in French under the title *Le Temps d'un Soupir*. Copyright © 1963 by Rene Julliard. Reprinted with the permission of Atheneum Publishers.

Barnstone, Willis, author: "Disappearance." Copyright © 1982 by Willis Barnstone. Reprinted by permission of the author.

Beacon Press: Jane Burgess Kohn and Willard K. Kohn, from *The Widower*. Copyright © 1978 by Jane Burgess Kohn and Willard K. Kohn. Reprinted by permission of Beacon Press.

Curtis Brown, Ltd.: Denise Jallais, "Lullaby for My Dead Child," from *A Book of Women Poets*, translated from French by Maxine Kumin and Judith Kumin. English translation copyright © 1980 by Maxine Kumin and Judith Kumin. Reprinted by permission of Curtis Brown, Ltd.

lished by Martin Secker & Warburg Limited, London, England. Reprinted by permission of Farrar, Straus and Giroux, Inc. and Martin Secker & Warburg Limited. Toby Talbot, selection from *A Book About My Mother.* Copyright © 1980 by Toby Talbot. Reprinted by permission of Farrar, Straus and Giroux, Inc. Edmund Wilson, selection from *The Thirties,* edited with an introduction by Leon Edel. Copyright © 1980 by Helen Miranda Wilson. Copyright © 1980 by Leon Edel. Reprinted by permission of Farrar, Straus and Giroux, Inc.

George, Phil, author: "The Visit," from *Voices of the Rainbow: Contemporary Poetry by American Indians,* edited by Kenneth Rosen (New York: Viking Press, 1975). Copyright © Phil George. Reprinted by permission of the author.

Grosset & Dunlap, Inc.: James Agee, selections from *A Death in the Family.* Copyright © 1957 by the James Agee Trust. Reprinted by permission of Grosset & Dunlap, Inc.

Harcourt Brace Jovanovich, Inc.: Selection from *The Diary of Virginia Woolf, Volume 3,* edited by Anne Oliver Bell, 1980, published by Harcourt Brace Jovanovich. Reprinted by permission of Harcourt Brace Jovanovich,

Inc. and the author's literary estate and the Hogarth Press Ltd. Ruth Stone, "Being Human," from *Topography and Other Poems.* Copyright © 1971 by Ruth Stone. Reprinted by permission of Harcourt Brace Jovanovich, Inc. and the author. Ruth Stone, "Wild Asters" from *Topography and Other Poems.* Copyright © 1967 by Ruth Stone. Reprinted by permission of Harcourt Brace Jovanovich, Inc. and the author.

Harper & Row, Publishers, Inc.: Pearl S. Buck, specified excerpts from pp. 180–81, 225–27 in *A Bridge for Passing* by Pearl S. Buck (John Day Co.). Copyright © 1961, 1962 by Pearl S. Buck. Reprinted by permission of Harper & Row, Publishers, Inc. John Gunther, specified material from pp. 253, 258–60 in *Death Be Not Proud* by John Gunther. Copyright © 1949 by John Gunther. Reprinted by permission of Harper & Row Publishers, Inc. Charles Neider, specified material from *The Autobiography of Mark Twain* by Charles Neider. Copyright © 1959 by Charles Neider. Reprinted by permission of Harper & Row Publishers, Inc. Joseph Von Eichendorff, "On My Child's Death" by Joseph Von Eichendorff from *After Experience* by W. D. Snodgrass. Copyright © 1960 by W. D. Snodgrass. Reprinted by permission of Harper & Row Publishers, Inc.

Hartman, Linda, author: selections from *The Day After Death.* Copyright © 1982 by Linda Hartman. Reprinted by permission of the author.

Harvard University Press: Poem #607, from *The Complete Poems of Emily Dickinson.* Reprinted by permission of the publishers and the Trustees of Amherst College from *The Poems of Emily Dickinson,* edited by Thomas H. Johnson (Cambridge, Mass.: The Belknap Press of Harvard University Press). Copyright 1951, © 1955, 1979 by the President and the Fellows of Harvard College.

Holt, Rinehart and Winston: Robert Frost, "Home Burial," from *The Poetry of Robert Frost,* edited by Edward Connery Lathem. Copyright 1930, 1939, © 1969 by Holt, Rinehart and Winston. Copyright © 1958 by Robert

In memory of

Jack Moffat
1925–1979
and
Robert Pitts
1905–1980

and dedicated to their strong survivors:
Peter and Michael Moffat
Bill Moffat
John and Mary Moffat
Esther Laakso Pitts

In the midst of winter, I finally learned that there was in me an invincible summer.

—Albert Camus, *Actuelles*

Contents

SUMMER AND FALL

Introduction

A book should serve as an axe for the frozen sea
within us.
                                        —Franz Kafka

This book is a gathering from world literature of the words of
those who have survived the death of someone they love. Across
the centuries, from the raw emotions of private journals to the
distillations of poetry, the writers speak of the pain of grief and
describe their process through the spiral of mourning. I hope
what they have written will help break through the frozen sea
in readers who find themselves in sorrow, and will enable those
who would help the bereaved to understand some of grief's
contradictions. I also hope their words will prepare readers who
have not yet suffered such a loss for the nature of the journey to
a new self that mourning calls forth.

Although the selections focus on separation by death, I
believe they also apply to other forms of loss any of us might
endure in a lifetime.

The collection grew from my own need for such a resource
when a long and contented marriage ended with my husband's
sudden death. When I emerged from the first weeks of dazed
disbelief, I struggled to understand the bewildering range of emotions I was experiencing, from anger to despair. I also felt the
age-old need for the solemnity of a significant mourning ritual,
for some form that might impose order on these chaotic feelings.

We live in a culture poor in meaningful rite or ceremony.
My husband's simple memorial service was consistent with what
my sons and I thought would have been his wishes; but it did
not persuade me that he was truly dead, or that a passage of such
significance to me had been sufficiently honored. Outwardly, I
appeared to be managing well, continuing my teaching, settling
financial matters, trying to take care of the emotional needs of

those who wanted to care for me. I was, in short, performing the role the outer world admires of one who is "taking it very well." But this façade is in exact contradiction to what psychologists say is necessary to complete successfully the task of mourning, in which all aspects of the loss must be expressed and worked through. Grief repressed, we're told, will exact a price, often years later. Caught between these conflicting messages, I perceived that I was facing the greatest challenge of my life.

As I went through the dreary task of answering condolence letters, I found enclosed in one note the quotation from Albert Camus that serves as the title of this book and which spoke to that challenge. These were the first words of solace I'd been able to comprehend, partly because they did not try to comfort or explain. Not only was recovery something I must accomplish myself but it was in the imagery of literature, which expresses the processes at work in human life and death in ways that can't be explained rationally, that I might find confirmation of my own emotions in a way that only can be called spiritual.

Literature is one of the few resources we have in modern times for living the deep life and not being simply spectators of our own experience. Love, loss and death, of course, have always been its great themes, and a lifetime of reading has given me some knowledge of their complexities. But we can draw from books only that which we already know. The poet's intuitive gift for finding hidden likenesses in things in the objective world that correspond to our psychic life stirs and awakens in a special way the emotions of those who feel wordless in the face of loss.

Even familiar literature took on new meaning for me. As I read and reread what writers both distinguished and little known have said about sorrow, I looked in particular for writing that revealed inner feelings unacceptable to the outer world, that avoided easy sentiments or consolations in favor of hard, often brutal truths. If it is important to feel every nuance of the pain of severance, then it was fortunate that in the private act of reading I was able to reexperience my own hurt as I journeyed with others through theirs.

In my search for these hard truths, I read in no systematic way. Poetry, with its capacity to illuminate a single intense moment in the life of the writer, helped to isolate and untangle the many strands of my own knot of feelings. For the slow progress of individual griefs, with the doubling back and forth between signs of recovery and setbacks, I searched out private journals kept by writers who use the language well. Because the journals were written initially to aid the writers' catharsis, they don't censor any facet of grief's self-absorption or the need to repeat over and over again the dimensions of loss before it can be accepted.

As I read, I realized that I might perform some service to others if I assembled these varying voices in an arrangement that suggested how differently individuals manage their grief, yet at the same time how, for most of us, grief runs a fairly predictable course. A commitment to the concerns of the larger community is a sign of revival for one in mourning. The idea that the literature that moved and reassured me might also help others became a turning point in my own process of recovery.

To offer readers relief from the emotional intensity of the poetry and journals, I have included excerpts from memoirs by writers like Pearl Buck and Daphne du Maurier, who look back on their grief from the vantage point of wisdom. These evaluative views show that not only is it possible to survive but we can be made stronger by our loss.

I felt that juxtaposing a variety of literary forms best revealed the interplay of light and dark in the many aspects of mourning. The greater distance from grief achieved by fiction writers allows us to stand back and look at bereavement with perspective. The selections from the partly autobiographical novels of James Agee and William Maxwell demonstrate how the lifelong impact of a death in the family is transformed by gifted writers into narrative art. It's an accident, I think, that three of the four short stories I've chosen to reprint in their entirety are by writers of Irish background, but perhaps not. Along with Russian story writers, represented here by Anton Chekhov, the Irish traditionally have excelled at capturing the complications

xxvi   Introduction

of the human condition in the space of a few pages, and, as in
Frank O'Connor's "Requiem," finding poignant humor, even in
sorrow.

   In arranging the collection, I've used the images of nature
and the seasons that are expressed repeatedly in literature to describe the recurring cycles of grief. The persistence over the centuries of seasonal imagery as an analogy for the swings of emotions
in bereavement from extreme sorrow to reconciliation suggests a
profound psychic need to come to terms with the violent and unpredictable forces of nature, and ultimately to find some reassuring pattern of renewal underlying that disorder.*
   The winter of early grief, as seen by the writers in the first
section, is a vision of a cosmos devoid of meaning. It is the world
that has died, not the beloved. Nature is indifferent to our sorrow, and the beauty of a spring the dead one is not here to enjoy
is more an insult than an affirmation.
   Metaphorically, spring is the period of great despair and
yearning, the phase of searching for that lost aspect of ourselves
the dead represent. It is this pull between the future and the past
that places the mourner in such a precarious position. As Lady
Ise, a ninth-century Japanese poet, says, there is "nothing left to
cling to." The work of this season of mourning is to incorporate
what is precious in the past and in our memory of the dead person into our living selves. When this is accomplished, we allow
ourselves to be pulled with the seasons into a summer of acceptance, when nature is imbued with meaning because we understand both heartbreak and renewal. It is then that survivors are
prepared for an autumn in which we are able to view with
equanimity the prospect of our own death.
   Mark Twain points out that the human mind cannot en-
compass immediately the profound implications of all that has
been lost; and in this arrangement of selections through the seasons of grief, there is considerable overlapping of emotional

* For a study of changing historical attitudes toward death and nature, see
Philippe Aries, *The Hour of Our Death,* Alfred A. Knopf, 1981.

material, just as the progress of a grief loops back and forth in
ever-widening circles. Grief is not tidy. It would be a mistake
to impose expectations of fixed "stages" or schedules on such a
complex and individual process. My concern about appearing to
impose too neat a structure on grief's disorders is lessened by the
knowledge that few of us read an anthology straight through as
narrative. Indeed, I like to imagine readers skipping ahead to
the more transcendent views in the section titled "Summer" for
reassurance, going back to the earlier expressions of pain to fully
discharge their own.

I found myself reassured by these writings that for many
survivors the weight of loss is carried longer than the traditional
year. The sensation of the heaviness of sorrow is an image that
goes back to the ancients; the root of the word *grieve* is *heavy*.
It is as if we must carry the dead as a cherished burden until we
are willing, finally, to let them go. Many months after my husband died, I asked a friend who had been widowed several years
when I might expect to feel less heavy-hearted.

He answered, "After you stop saying 'last year at this time.'
After you stop saying, 'we' and 'our.'" The men and women in
this book confirm that recovery is not a process we can will, but
consists of experiencing many small deaths, the passing of significant anniversaries, until our identity is solid and natural in
the pronoun "I."

To me, the most paradoxical of these many symbolic deaths
is the passing of grief itself. Feeling better, more frequently
"surprised by joy," as was Wordsworth, I also felt a sense of betrayal of my husband, even though I rationally knew that sustained grief would be morbid. Because grief may become a
substitute for the dead one, giving up our grief can be the greatest
challenge of mourning. If many of the journals, such as the one
kept by Anne Philipe, conclude on this ambivalent note, we
should not assume it is because the grief remains unresolved.
Rather, at this point, there was less need to write.

If these selections offer some illumination into the mourning process, let me remind readers how much more there is for

us in the classics of the past and in distinguished contemporary writing on this eternal subject. Each day I come across work of emotional honesty and literary distinction it is now too late to include. But just as C. S. Lewis vowed not to write any more about his grief when the last copybook in the house was filled, I'm grateful that the publication deadline has imposed an arbitrary ending on my excavations. It's time for me to move on.

I do so in the knowledge that I've left unexamined the literature of many cultures and periods. But my reading has persuaded me that although religious customs, social mores and psychological interpretations vary, over the centuries human sorrow has felt much the same. In choosing the poetry, I responded to work that was direct and personal in its expression of pain and that I felt would be immediately accessible to others in this emotional state. The many beautiful formal elegies that grace our literary heritage are, I think, more rewarding for readers in a later stage of mourning than I was in when I began this compilation. I hope that some of the more familiar works I've included will yield fresh meaning in their setting, as an art exhibit arranged around a specific theme enables us to see old masters in a new way.

At a recent exhibit of American quilts at the Oakland Art Museum I was moved by an example titled "Widow's Quilt." The artist had fashioned from her husband's clothes a tableau of their life together. Around certain scenes—their wedding day, the gravestone of a child—her usually meticulous patching veered, the uneven stitches a powerful metaphor for her grief. By assembling from the fabric of memory all that had been lost, all she still cherished, she created a comforter of warmth for others and a work of enduring beauty. The quiltmaker and the writers in this book suggest that each of us might create, in our own way, something new from sorrow. In that spirit, I offer this collection in tribute to all who have mourned.

Winter

Winter under cultivation
Is as arable as spring.

—Emily Dickinson

"And can it be that in a world so full and busy,
the loss of one weak creature makes a void in
any heart, so wide and deep that nothing but the
width and depth of vast eternity can fill it up!"
—Charles Dickens, *Dombey and Son*

Shock

The shock of first grief is an amazement that what was alive and of this world only a few moments ago is irrevocably gone. The writers in the next selections focus on very specific images as a mooring to reality in the face of this vanishing.

Stanley Moss

For Margaret

My mother near her death
is white as a downy feather.
I used to think her death was as distant
as a tropical bird,
a giant macaw, whatever that is—
a thing I have as little to do with
as the distant poor.
I find a single feather of her suffering,
I blow it gently as she blew
into my neck and ear.

A single downy feather is on the scales,
opposed of things of weight, not spirit.
I remember the smell of burning feathers.
I wish we could sit upon the grass
and talk about grandchildren
and great-grandchildren.
A worm directs us into the ground.
We look alike.

I sing a lullaby to her about her children,
who are safe, and their children.

I place a Venetian lace tablecloth
on the grass of the whitest linen.
The wind comes with its song
about things given that are taken away
and given again in another form.

Why are the poor cawing, hooting,
screaming in the woods?
I wish death were a whippoorwill.
Why is everything so heavy?
I did not think
she was still helping me carry
the weight of my life.
Now the world's poor are before me.
How can I lift them one by one in my arms?

Stan Rice

Rice and his wife, novelist Anne Rice, lost their daughter to
leukemia when she was six.

Look!

Look! she is dead: no cover can cover her: look,
her hands are dead just as her face is dead: all of her is dead:
where is the soul? she looked no lighter on the pillow when it
      went.
My eyes fill with water that falls from under my sunglasses:
when the bells ring: even the oxygen grieves:
surely this is not what she was meant for:
look! a shaft of light pierces the dustball: just that effortlessly

she went.

Adelaide Crapsey
1878–1914

Triad

These be
Three silent things:
The falling snow . . . the hour
Before the dawn . . . the mouth of one
Just dead.

Witter Bynner
1881–1968

Death of a Friend

I had not known, in friendly life attached,
That death cleaves suddenly yet leaves two legs
That both still bear their weight, two legs still matched
And walking still among the ashen dregs.
I had not known that the body bore so much,
That so bereaved it still would walk and thrive:
I had not known that, with no sense of touch,
An individual could stay alive.

Mark Twain
1835–1910

Mark Twain's vocation was "to excite the laughter of God's
creatures" through his writing. In private life, as Samuel Clemens,

he endured many sorrows. By his own admission, his twenty-two-month-old son died from his father's neglect when he took him for a carriage ride, "fell into a reverie," and let the child's covers fall away, exposing him to the freezing cold; his favorite daughter, Susy, died suddenly of meningitis; his wife, Olivia, suffered an extended period of mental illness after Susy's death and died just as she seemed to be on the verge of recovery. Five years later his daughter Jean died of a heart attack during an epileptic seizure.

In his *Autobiography* he wrote of the way the human mind fragments the impact of a great grief:

I was standing in our dining room, thinking of nothing in particular, when a cablegram was put in my hand. It said, "Susy was peacefully released to-day."

It is one of the mysteries of our nature that a man, all unprepared, can receive a thunderstroke like that and live. There is but one reasonable explanation of it. The intellect is stunned by the shock and but gropingly gathers the meaning of the words. The power to realize their full import is mercifully wanting. The mind has a dim sense of vast loss—that is all. It will take mind and memory months and possibly years to gather the details and thus learn and know the whole extent of the loss. A man's house burns down. The smoking wreckage represents only a ruined home that was dear through years of use and pleasant associations. By and by, as the days and weeks go on, first he misses this, then that, then the other thing. And when he casts about for it he finds that it was in that house. Always it is an *essential* —there was but one of its kind. It cannot be replaced. It was in that house. It is irrevocably lost. He did not realize that it was an essential when he had it; he only discovers it now when he finds himself balked, hampered, by its absence. It will be years before the tale of lost essentials is complete, and not till then can he truly know the magnitude of his disaster.

[After his daughter Jean's death in 1909 and four months before his own:]

Would I bring her back to life if I could do it? I would not. If a word would do it, I would beg for strength to withhold the word. And I would have the strength; I am sure of it. In her loss I am almost bankrupt, and my life is a bitterness, but I am content: for she has been enriched with that most precious of all gifts—that gift which makes all other gifts mean and poor—death. I have never wanted any released friend of mine restored to life since I reached manhood. I felt in this way when Susy passed away; and later my wife, and later Mr. Rogers. When Clara met me at the station in New York and told me Mr. Rogers had died suddenly that morning, my thought was, Oh, favorite of fortune—fortunate all his long and lovely life—fortunate to his latest moment! The reporters said there were tears of sorrow in my eyes. True—but they were for *me*, not for him. He had suffered no loss. All the fortunes he had ever made before were poverty compared with this one.

Lady Ise
875?–938?

A lady-in-waiting for Emperor Uda's consort, Onshi, Lady Ise spent her adult life at court and was about thirty-two years old when she wrote this elegy, with its images expressing the uncertainty of grief.

Elegy: Ise Lamenting the Death of Empress Onshi

The waves surge higher still
far off:
within the palace

Ise the diver
who has long lived there
feels her home-ship
swept away,
nothing left to cling to;
grief overcomes her.
Our tears are like
scarlet-tinged
autumn rain.
And like the maple leaves
of autumn, when the members
of the household
have scattered
in their own ways,
uncertainty
fills the air.
We who stayed behind
are like the pampas flowers
in a garden without a keeper.
We huddle together
and beckon to the sky:
the first wild geese of the season
cry out as they fly off,
indifferent to us.

Translated from the Japanese by Etsuko Terasaki
with Irma Brandeis

James Agee
1909–1955

Agee's posthumously published novel, *A Death in the Family*, is set in Knoxville, Tennessee, and is based on his own father's death, when the novelist was six. It provides a classic text on fresh grief as Agee explores the varying feelings of the entire family in the three days following Jay Follet's fatal car accident. In this selection, Mary Follet is dressing for her husband's funeral. Even in numbed shock, she registers the complicated waves of emotion felt by the newly bereaved, including a pride at her involuntary election into the historical community of mourners.

---

from *A Death in the Family*

When grief and shock surpass endurance there occur phases of exhaustion, of anesthesia in which relatively little is left and one has the illusion of recognizing, and understanding, a good deal. Throughout these days Mary had, during these breathing spells, drawn a kind of solace from the recurrent thought: at least I am enduring it. I am aware of what has happened, I am meeting it face to face, I am living through it. There had been, even, a kind of pride, a desolate kind of pleasure, in the feeling: I am carrying a heavier weight than I could have dreamed it possible for a human being to carry, yet I am living through it. It had of course occurred to her that this happens to many people, that it is very common, and she humbled and comforted herself in this thought. She thought: this is simply what living is; I never realized before what it is. She thought: now I am more nearly a grown member of the human race; bearing children, which had seemed so much, was just so much apprenticeship. She thought that she had never before had a chance to realize the strength that human beings have, to endure; she loved and revered all those who had ever suffered, even those who had failed to endure. She thought that she had never before had a chance to realize the might, grimness and tenderness of God. She thought that now for the first time she began to know herself, and she gained extraordinary hope in this beginning of knowledge. She thought that she had almost grown up overnight. She thought that she had realized all that was in her soul to realize in the event, and when at length the time came to put on her veil, leave the bed-

room she had shared with her husband, leave their home, and
go down to see him for the first time since his death and to see
the long day through, which would cover him out of sight for
the duration of this world, she thought that she was firm and
ready. She had refused to "try on" her veil; the mere thought of
approving or disapproving it before a mirror was obscene; so
now when she came to the mirror and drew it down across her
face to go, she saw herself for the first time since her husband's
death. Without either desiring to see her face, or caring how it
looked, she saw that it had changed; through the deep, clear veil
her gray eyes watched her gray eyes watch her through the deep,
clear veil. I must have fever, she thought, startled by their bright-
ness; and turned away. It was when she came to the door, to
walk through it, to leave this room and to leave this shape of
existence forever, that realization poured upon and overwhelmed
her through which, in retrospect, she would one day know all
that had gone before, all that she had thought she experienced
and knew—true, more or less, though it all was—was nothing
to this. The realization came without shape or definability, save
as it was focused in the pure physical acts of leaving the room,
but came with such force, such monstrous piercing weight, in all
her heart and soul and mind and body but above all in the womb,
where it arrived and dwelt like a cold and prodigious, spreading
stone, that groaned almost inaudibly, almost a mere silent breath,
an *Ohhhhhh*, and doubled deeply over, hands to her belly, and
her knee joints melted.

Gaius Valerius Catullus
84?–54 B.C.

On the Burial of His Brother

By ways remote and distant waters sped,
  Brother, to thy sad graveside am I come,

That I may give the last gifts to the dead,
  And vainly parley with thine ashes dumb;
Since She who now bestows and now denies
  Hath ta'en thee, hapless brother, from mine eyes.
But lo! these gifts, the heirlooms of past years,
  Are made sad things to grace thy coffin-shell;
Take them, all drenchèd with a brother's tears,
  And, brother, for all time, hail and farewell.

Translated from the Greek by Aubrey Beardsley

THE HOLY BIBLE
(King James Version)

from the Second Book of Samuel (12:18–23)

The life of one who mourns is always itself in jeopardy. Preoccupation with loss leads us to neglect our health. Food has no savor when we are starved for the nourishment of our severed affections. In the Old Testament, after the death of the son born to his beloved Bathsheba, King David set an example of acceptance of the claims of life in the face of unchangeable loss.

And it came to pass on the seventh day, that the child died. And the servants of David feared to tell him that the child was dead: for they said, Behold, while the child was yet alive, we spake unto him, and he would not hearken unto our voice: how will he then vex himself, if we tell him that the child is dead?

But when David saw that his servants whispered, David said unto his servants, Is the child dead? And they said, He is dead.

Then David rose from the earth, and washed, and anointed himself, and changed his apparel, and came into the house of the Lord, and worshipped; then he came to his own house; and when he required, they set bread before him, and he did eat.

Then said his servants unto him, What thing is this that thou hast done? thou didst fast and weep for the child, while it was alive; but when the child was dead, thou didst rise and eat bread.

And he said, While the child was yet alive, I fasted and wept: for I said, Who can tell whether God will be gracious to me, that the child may live?

But now he is dead, wherefore should I fast? can I bring him back again? I shall go to him, but he shall not return to me.

Idealization and Anger

In the period of early shock, the mourner may idealize the dead. In the process of searching for the lost perfection, nature and the living are devalued, often with considerable anger.

William Shakespeare
1564–1616

from *Antony and Cleopatra*

Cleopatra: Noblest of men, woo't die?
           Hast thou no care of me? Shall I abide
           In this dull world, which in thy absence is
           No better than a sty? O, see, my women
                       (Antony dies)
           the crown o' the earth doth melt. My lord!
           O, wither'd is the garland of the war,
           The soldier's pole is fall'n! Young boys and girls
           Are level now with men; the odds is gone,
           And there is nothing left remarkable
           Beneath the visiting moon.

                             Act V, Scene 1

Elinor Wylie
1885–1928

Little Elegy

Withouten you
No rose can grow;
No leaf be green
If never seen
Your sweetest face;
No bird have grace
Or power to sing;
Or anything
Be kind, or fair,
And you nowhere.

Jose Luis Hidalgo
1919–1947

No

The night crushes you so I look for you
like a maniac in shadow, in a dream, in death.
My heart burns up like a single bird.
Your absence murders me, life has closed.

What loneliness, what darkness, what a parched moon goes by,
what distant people are looking for your lost body.
They ask your blood, your lips, your sound,
your inseparable absence in the growing night.

My hands don't hold you and my eyes miss you.
My words look for you on foot, uselessly.

Inside me the quiet night is long, lies down,
stretches like a river whose banks are alone.

But I go on looking for you, digging you up, dissolving you
in shadow, in a dream. I nail you down in memory.
Silence creates your unsayable truth.
The world has closed. For me, permanently.

Translated from the Spanish by Stephen Berg

Kenneth Patchen
1911–1972

Kathleen was the poet's youngest sister who was killed at the age of ten when an automobile jumped the sidewalk and struck her.

In Memory of Kathleen

How pitiful is her sleep.
Now her clear breath is still.

There is nothing falling tonight,
Bird or man,
As dear as she.

Nowhere that she should go
Without me. None but my calling.

O nothing but the cold cry of the snow.

Orlando Gibbons
1583–1625

The Silver Swan

The silver swan, who, living had no note,
When death approached, unlocked her silent throat;
Leaning her breast against the reedy shore,
Thus sang her first and last, and sang no more.
Farewell all joys. O death come close my eyes,
More geese than swans now live, more fools than wise.

Amy Lowell
1874–1925

From One Who Stays

How empty seems the town now you are gone!
   A wilderness of sad streets, where gaunt walls
   Hide nothing to desire; sunshine falls
Eery, distorted, as it long had shone
On white, dead faces tombed in halls of stone.
   The whir of motors, stricken through with calls
   Of playing boys, floats up at intervals;
But all these noises blur to one long moan.
   What quest is worth pursuing? And how strange
That other men still go accustomed ways!
I hate their interest in the things they do.
   A spectre-horde repeating without change.

Edna St. Vincent Millay
1892–1950

Millay's twenty-six-year marriage to the supportive Eugen Jan Boissevain ended with his death in 1949. For many years in precarious health, she died of a heart attack the following year.

Dirge Without Music

I am not resigned to the shutting away of loving hearts in the
    hard ground.
So it is, and so it will be, for so it has been time out of mind:
Into the darkness they go, the wise and the lovely. Crowned
With lilies and with laurel they go; but I am not resigned.

Lovers and thinkers, into the earth with you,
Be one with the dull, the indiscriminate dust.
A fragment of what you felt, of what you knew,
A formula, a phrase remains—but the best is lost.

The answers quick and keen, the honest look, the laughter,
    the love—
They are gone. They are gone to feed the roses. Elegant and
    curled
Is the blossom. Fragrant is the blossom. I know. But I do
    not approve.
More precious was the light in your eyes than all the roses of the
    world.

Down, down, down into the darkness of the grave
Gently they go, the beautiful, the tender, the kind;
Quietly they go, the intelligent, the witty, the brave.
I know. But I do not approve. And I am not resigned.

Nell Altizer

The Widow Teaches Poetry Writing

Over and over again I order my students
out to the graveyards to find their poems.

Any old line, I say, the slug, the kicked down
pot, spurge, condom, wreath, the nest of lizards in the

weeds, the grave-keeper's mildewed teeth,
even (if you must) the long limousines of silence.

And you over there, yes, *you*, tell me the
story of your Chinese grandmother's duties,

How after seven years she must dig the bones
of her husband's father out of the ground

And wash them one by one in the clear
rain water and lay them to dry in the sun,

while her son's wife kneels down beside her
in the patient air, learning how it's done.

The boys and girls come back sweating
the words that say, shit, you hard bitch.

Their poems reek of fear and earthworms,
their faces smeared with hate for me,

Dis,
who has brought them young and early, young and
twitching to this place.

Sing Sorrow

The winter of first grief is a season of hushed quiet, the sound-lessness of new snow, a numbness that has no voice to sing sorrow. The next selections address the mourner's need to break that silence, from the cool meditation of French essayist Michel de Montaigne to the compassionate understanding of the great Russian writer Anton Chekhov, in his short story of a bereaved cab driver and his horse.

Michel de Montaigne
1533–1592

from *The Essays*

OF SADNESS

The story says that Psammenitus, King of Egypt, having been defeated and captured by Cambyses, King of Persia, seeing his daughter pass by, a prisoner, dressed as a servant sent to draw water, all his friends around him weeping and lamenting, stood motionless and silent, his eyes fixed on the ground; and soon after, seeing his son led to death, he maintained the same demeanour. But, having perceived one of his household among the captives, he beat his head and gave way to extreme lamentation. This might be coupled with what we recently saw to be the case with one of our princes, who, having heard at Trent, where he was, of the death of his eldest brother—a brother upon whom, indeed, rested the support and honour of his family—and very soon afterward of the death of a younger brother, its next hope; and having sustained these two assaults with exemplary firmness, when, some days later, one of his servants died, he allowed himself to be overcome by this last event, and, losing all his self-control, abandoned himself to mourning and regret, in such a way that it was argued by some that he had been touched to the quick only by the last blow; but the truth was that, when Cambyses asked Psammenitus why it was that, not being moved by the unhappy fate of his son and his daughter, he bore with so little patience that of his friend, "Because," he replied, "only that last grief could be shewn by tears; the first two far surpassed all means of expression." Perhaps, in this connection, we might recall the conceit of that ancient painter, who, having to represent the mourning of those present at the sacrifice of Iphigenia according to the degree of each person's interest in the death of that innocent fair maid, having exhausted the last resources of his art, when it came to the maiden's father, he painted him with his face covered, as if no visage could evince that degree of grief. This is why poets described that wretched mother Niobe, when she had lost, first, seven sons, and straightway as many daughters, over-burdened with her losses, as having at last been transformed to stone—

As having been petrified by calamity,*

to express that sombre, dumb, and deaf torpor that paralyses us when events surpassing our capability overwhelm us. In truth, the effect of an affliction, if it be extreme, must wholly stun the mind and deprive it of freedom of action; as, on the startling alarm of some very ill news, it happens to us to feel dazed and deadened, and, as it were, completely paralysed, in such wise that the mind, upon giving way later to tears and lamentations, seems to relax and disperse itself, and take a wider sweep, more at its ease.

And at last, with difficulty, a passage
for words is opened by grief.†

Translated from the French by George B. Ives

* Ovid, *Metamorphoses*, VI, 304.
† Vergil, *Aeneid*, XI, 151.

Elizabeth Barrett Browning
1806–1861

Grief

I tell you, hopeless grief is passionless;
    That only men incredulous of despair,
    Half-taught in anguish, through the midnight air
Beat upward to God's throne in loud access
Of shrieking and reproach. Full desertness,
    In souls as countries, lieth silent-bare
    Under the blanching, vertical eye-glare
Of the absolute Heavens. Deep-hearted man, express
Grief for thy Dead in silence like to death—
    Most like a monumental statue set
In everlasting watch and moveless woe
Till itself crumble to dust beneath.
    Touch it; the marble eyelids are not wet:
If it could weep, it could arise and go.

Seneca
4 B.C.–A.D. 65

from *Hippolytus*

Light griefs can speak; great ones are dumb.

Act II, Scene 3

John Dryden
1631–1700

from *Threnodia Augustalis*

Sure there's a lethargy in mighty woe;
   Tears stand congealed and cannot flow,
And the sad soul retires into her inmost room.
Tears for a stroke foreseen afford relief.
   But unprovided for a sudden blow,
   Like Niobe we marble grow
      And petrify with grief.

Samuel Taylor Coleridge
1772–1834

from Dejection

A grief without a pang, void, dark, and drear,
A drowsy, stifled, unimpassioned grief,
Which finds not natural outlet or relief
In word, or sigh, or tear.

William Shakespeare
1564–1616

from *Macbeth*

Give sorrow words; the grief that does
not speak whispers the oe'r fraught heart
and bids it break.

Alfred, Lord Tennyson
1809–1892

Immediately after the early death of his close friend Arthur
Hallam, who was engaged to his sister, Tennyson sought relief
in lyric utterance. The collection of lyrics, growing through
seventeen years, reads like a diary on the progress of a private
grief, with all its questionings and doubts, into an eventual
affirmation of love as the soul of the world. This selection is from
the first section of absorption in grief.

---

from *In Memoriam A.H.H.*

V

I sometimes hold it half a sin
   To put in words the grief I feel;
   For words, like Nature, half reveal
And half conceal the Soul within.

But, for the unquiet heart and brain,
   A use in measured language lies;
   The sad mechanic exercise,
Like dull narcotics, numbing pain.

In words, like weeds, I'll wrap me o'er,
   Like coarsest clothes against the cold;
   But that large grief which these enfold
Is given in outline and no more.

Anton Chekhov
1860–1904

Grief

"TO WHOM SHALL I TELL MY GRIEF?"

It is twilight. A thick wet snow is slowly twirling around the
newly lighted street-lamps, and lying in soft thin layers on the
roofs, the horses' backs, people's shoulders and hats. The cab-
driver, Iona Potapov, is quite white, and looks like a phantom;
he is bent double as far as a human body can bend double; he
is seated on his box, and never makes a move. If a whole snow-
drift fell on him, it seems as if he would not find it necessary to
shake it off. His little horse is also quite white, and remains
motionless; its immobility, its angularity, and its straight wooden-
looking legs, even close by give it the appearance of a ginger-
bread horse worth a kopeck. It is, no doubt, plunged in deep
thought. If you were snatched from the plough, from your usual
grey surroundings, and were thrown into this slough full of
monstrous lights, unceasing noise and hurrying people, you too
would find it difficult not to think.

Iona and his little horse have not moved from their place
for a long while. They left their yard before dinner, and, up to
now, not a "fare." The evening mist is descending over the town,
the white lights of the lamps are replacing brighter rays, and
the hubbub of the street is getting louder. "Cabby, for Viborg
way!" suddenly hears Iona. "Cabby!"

Iona jumps, and through his snow-covered eyelashes, sees
an officer in a greatcoat, with his hood over his head.

"Viborg way!" the officer repeats. "Are you asleep, eh?
Viborg way!"

With a nod of assent Iona picks up the reins, in conse-
quence of which layers of snow slip off the horse's back and
neck. The officer seats himself in the sleigh, the cab-driver
smacks his lips to encourage his horse, stretches out his neck

like a swan, sits up, and, more from habit than necessity, brandishes his whip. The little horse also stretches his neck, bends his wooden-looking legs, and makes a move undecidedly.

"What are you doing, were-wolf!" is the exclamation Iona hears, from the dark mass moving to and fro as soon as they started.

"Where the devil are you going? To the r-r-right!"

"You do not know how to drive. Keep to the right!" calls the officer angrily.

A coachman from a private carriage swears at him; a passer-by, who has run across the road and rubbed his shoulder against the horse's nose, looks at him furiously as he sweeps the snow from his sleeve. Iona shifts about on his seat as if he were on needles, moves his elbows as if he were trying to keep his equilibrium, and gapes about like someone suffocating, and who does not understand why and wherefore he is there.

"What scoundrels they all are!" jokes the officer; "one would think they had all entered into an agreement to jostle you or fall under your horse."

Iona looks round at the officer, and moves his lips. He evidently wants to say something, but the only sound that issues is a snuffle.

"What?" asks the officer.

Iona twists his mouth into a smile, and with an effort says hoarsely:

"My son, barin, died this week."

"Hm! What did he die of?"

Iona turns with his whole body towards his fare, and says:

"And who knows! They say high fever. He was three days in hospital, and then died. . . . God's will be done."

"Turn round! The devil!" sounded from the darkness. "Have you popped off, old doggie, eh? Use your eyes!"

"Go on, go on," said the officer, "otherwise we shall not get there by to-morrow. Hurry a bit!"

The cab-driver again stretches his neck, sits up, and, with

a bad grace, brandishes his whip. Several times again he turns to look at his fare, but the latter had closed his eyes, and apparently is not disposed to listen. Having deposited the officer in the Viborg, he stops by the tavern, doubles himself up on his seat, and again remains motionless, while the snow once more begins to cover him and his horse. An hour, and another. . . . Then, along the footpath, with a squeak of goloshes, and quarrelling, came three young men, two of them tall and lanky, the third one short and hump-backed.

"Cabby, to the Police Bridge!" in a cracked voice calls the hump-back. "The three of us for two griveniks!" (20 kopecks).

Iona picks up his reins, and smacks his lips. Two griveniks is not a fair price, but he does not mind if it is a rouble or five kopecks—to him it is all the same now, so long as they are wayfarers. The young men, jostling each other and using bad language, approach the sleigh, and all three at once try to get on to the seat; then begins a discussion which two shall sit and who shall be the one to stand. After wrangling, abusing each other, and much petulance, it was at last decided that the hump-back should stand, as he was the smallest.

"Now then, hurry up!" says the hump-back in a twanging voice, as he takes his place, and breathes in Iona's neck. "Old furry. Here, mate, what a cap you have got, there is not a worse one to be found in all Petersburg! . . ."

"Hi—hi,—hi—hi," giggles Iona. "Such a . . ."

"Now you, 'such a,' hurry up, are you going the whole way at this pace? Are you? . . . Do you want it in the neck?"

"My head feels like bursting," says one of the lanky ones. "Last night at the Donkmasovs, Vaska and I drank the whole of four bottles of cognac."

"I don't understand what you lie for," said the other lanky one angrily; "you lie like a brute."

"God strike me, it's the truth!"

"It's as much a truth as that a louse coughs!"

"Hi, hi," grins Iona, "what gay young gentlemen!"

"Pshaw, go to the devil!" indignantly says the hump-back.

"Are you going to get on or not, you old pest? Is that the way to drive? Use the whip a bit! Go on, devil, go on, give it him well!"

Iona feels at his back the little man wriggling, and the tremble in his voice. He listens to the insults hurled at him, sees the people, and little by little the feeling of loneliness leaves him. The hump-back goes on swearing until he gets mixed up in some elaborate six-foot oath, or chokes with coughing. The lankies begin to talk about a certain Nadejda Petrovna. Iona looks round at them several times; he waits for a temporary silence, then, turning round again, he murmurs:

"My son—died this week."

"We must all die," sighed the hump-back, wiping his lips after an attack of coughing. "Now, hurry up, hurry up! Gentlemen, I really cannot go any farther like this! When will he get us there?"

"Well, just you stimulate him a little in the neck!"

"You old pest, do you hear, I'll bone your neck for you! If one treated the like of you with ceremony one would have to go on foot! Do you hear, old serpent Gorinytch! Or do you not care a spit?"

Iona hears rather than feels the blows they deal him.

"Hi, hi," he laughs. "They are gay young gentlemen, God bless 'em!"

"Cabby, are you married?" asks a lanky one.

"I? Hi, hi, gay young gentlemen! Now I have only a wife: the moist ground. . . . Hi, ho, ho . . . that is to say, the grave! My son has died, and I am alive. . . . A wonderful thing, death mistook the door . . . instead of coming to me, it went to my son . . ."

Iona turns round to tell them how his son died, but at this moment the hump-back, giving a little sigh, announces, "Thank God, they have at last reached their destination," and Iona watches them disappear through the dark entrance. Once more he is alone, and again surrounded by silence. . . . His grief, which had abated for a short while, returns and rends his heart with greater force. With an anxious and a hurried look, he searches among the crowds passing on either side of the street to find if there is just one person who will listen to him. But the crowds hurry by without noticing him or his trouble. Yet it is such an immense, illimitable grief. Should his heart break and the grief pour out, it would flow over the whole earth it seems, and yet, no one sees it. It has managed to conceal itself in such an insignificant shell that no one can see it even by day and with a light.

Iona sees a hall-porter with some sacking, and decides to talk to him.

"Friend, what sort of time is it?" he asks.

"Past nine. What are you standing here for? Move on."

Iona moves on a few steps, doubles himself up, and abandons himself to his grief. He sees it is useless to turn to people for help. In less than five minutes he straightens himself, holds up his head as if he felt some sharp pain, and gives a tug at the reins: he can bear it no longer, "The stables," he thinks, and the little horse, as if he understood, starts off at a trot.

About an hour and a half later Iona is seated by a large dirty stove. Around the stove, on the floor, on the benches, people are snoring; the air is thick and suffocatingly hot. Iona looks at the sleepers, scratches himself, and regrets having returned so early.

"I have not even earned my fodder," he thinks. "That's what's my trouble. A man who knows his job, who has had enough to eat, and his horse too, can always sleep peacefully."

A young cab-driver in one of the corners half gets up, grunts sleepily, and stretches towards a bucket of water.

"Do you want a drink?" Iona asks him.

"Don't I want a drink!"

"That's so? Your good health! But listen, mate—you know, my son is dead. . . . Did you hear? This week, in hospital. . . . It's a long story."

Iona looks to see what effect his words have, but sees none
—the young man has hidden his face, and is fast asleep again.
The old man sighs, and scratches his head. Just as much as the
young one wanted to drink, the old man wanted to talk. It will
soon be a week since his son died, and he has not been able to
speak about it properly to anyone. One must tell it slowly and
carefully; how his son fell ill, how he suffered, what he said
before he died, how he died. One must describe every detail of
the funeral, and the journey to the hospital to fetch the defunct's
clothes. His daughter Anissia remained in the village—one must
talk about her too. Was it nothing he had to tell? Surely the
listener would gasp and sigh, and sympathise with him? It is
better, too, to talk to women; although they are stupid, two
words are enough to make them sob.

"I'll go and look at my horse," thinks Iona; "there's always
time to sleep. No fear of that!"

He puts on his coat, and goes to the stables to his horse;
he thinks of the corn, the hay, the weather. When he is alone,
he dare not think of his son; he could speak about him to anyone, but to think of him, and picture him to himself, is unbear-
ably painful.

"Are you tucking in?" Iona asks his horse, looking at his
bright eyes; "go on, tuck in, though we've not earned our corn,
we can eat hay. Yes! I am too old to drive—my son could have,
not I. He was a first-rate cab-driver. If only he had lived!"

Iona is silent for a moment, then continues:

"That's how it is, my old horse. There's no more Kuzma
Ionitch. He has left us to live, and he went off pop. Now let's
say, you had a foal, you were that foal's mother, and suddenly,
let's say, that foal went and left you to live after him. It would
be sad, wouldn't it?"

The little horse munches, listens, and breathes over his
master's hand. . . .

Iona's feelings are too much for him, and he tells the little
horse the whole story.

THE HOLY BIBLE
(King James Version)

from the Book of Lamentations (2:18)

. . . let tears run down like a river day and night: give thyself
no rest; let not the apple of thine eye cease.

THE HOLY BIBLE
(King James Version)

from the Book of Psalms (126:5–6)

They that sow in tears shall reap in joy.

He that goeth forth and weepeth, bearing precious seed,
shall doubtless come again with rejoicing, bringing his sheaves
with him.

Consolations

Those who haven't experienced bereavement often find themselves at a loss to offer words of consolation. Chekhov's story shows that words may be less important than sympathetic listening. Any form of acknowledgment is better than none at all. The next selections address the obligation of the community to understand and allow mourners to feel their pain rather than evade it.

Phillips Brooks
1835–1893

from a letter to his friend on the death of his mother, November 19, 1891

May I try to tell you again where your only comfort lies? It is not in forgetting the happy past. People bring us well-meant but miserable consolations when they tell us what time will do to help our grief. We do not want to lose our grief, because our grief is bound up with our love and we could not cease to mourn without being robbed of our affections.

Samuel Johnson
1709–1784

from James Boswell's *Life of Dr. Johnson*

While grief is fresh, every attempt to divert only irritates.

Elizabeth Cleghorn Gaskell
1810–1865

from *Cranford*

One gives people in grief their own way.

THE HOLY BIBLE
(King James Version)

from the Book of Ecclesiastes (7:2)

It is better to go to the house of mourning, than to go to the
house of feasting: for that is the end of all men; and the living
will lay it to his heart.

Maimonides
1135–1204

from the *Code*

LAWS CONCERNING MOURNING

It seems to me that the duty of comforting mourners takes pre-
cedence over the duty of visiting the sick, because comforting
mourners is an act of benevolence toward the living and the
dead.

Marcel Proust
1871–1922

from *Letters*

. . . there is no more ridiculous custom than the one that makes you express sympathy once and for all on a given day to a person whose sorrow will endure as long as his life. Such grief, felt in such a way is always "present," it is never too late to talk about it, never repetitious to mention it again.

Rabbi Meir

from *The Babylonian Talmud, Mo'ed Katan*

A person who meets a mourner after a year and speaks words of consolation to him then, to what can he be compared?

To a physician who meets a person whose leg had been broken and healed, and says to him, "Let me break your leg again, and reset it, to convince you that my treatment was good."

William Shakespeare
1564–1616

from *King John*

King Philip: You are as fond of grief as of your child.
Constance: Grief fills the room up of my absent child,
              Lies in his bed, walks up and down with me,
              Puts on his pretty looks, repeats his words,
              Remembers me of all his gracious parts,
              Stuffs out his vacant garments with his form;

Then, have I reason to be fond of grief?
Fare you well: had you such a loss as I,
I could give better comfort than you do.

Act III, Sc. 4

Marcel Proust
1871–1922

from *Letters*

And it is helpful, if one has the courage, to give people who are
suffering the kind of understanding that, by the time they have
changed, will appear to have been criticism. . . .

Isadora Duncan
1878–1927

Duncan lost both her young children when a taxicab in which
they were riding fell in the water and they were drowned. After
their death she fled to her friend, the Italian actress Eleonora
Duse, at Duse's villa in Italy. Duse did not offer Isadora Duncan
easy or trite prescriptions for her enormous loss. She allowed
Duncan to feel what had happened her, surely the most tender
and generous gesture of consolation.

from *My Life*

The next morning I drove out to see Duse, who was living in a
rose-coloured villa behind a vineyard. She came down a vine-

covered walk to meet me, like a glorious angel. She took me in her arms and her wonderful eyes beamed upon me such love and tenderness that I felt just as Dante must have felt when, in the "Paradiso," he encounters the Divine Beatrice.

From then on I lived at Viareggio, finding courage from the radiance of Eleanora's eyes. She used to rock me in her arms, consoling my pain, but not only consoling, for she seemed to take my sorrow to her own breast, and I realized that if I had not been able to bear the society of other people, it was because they all played the comedy of trying to cheer me with forgetfulness. Whereas Eleanora said:

"Tell me about Deirdre and Patrick," and made me repeat to her all their little sayings and ways, and show her their photos, which she kissed and cried over. She never said, "Cease to grieve," but she grieved with me, and, for the first time since their death, I felt I was not alone.

Grief's Distractions

While often it is impossible, and indeed unwise, to distract the bereaved from their loss, there are individuals who possess an irrepressible buoyancy of spirit that erupts even in the keen sorrow of fresh grief. Two great French novelists describe how their psyches protect such spirits by allowing a few moments of forgetfulness—the savoring of the present moment of just being alive: Marcel Proust in his fictional rendering of the father of his friend Swann, and Colette in her autobiographical recollection of her mother, Sido.

Marcel Proust
1871–1922

from *Remembrance of Things Past*

Several times in the course of a year I would hear my grandfather tell at table the story, which never varied, of the behaviour of M. Swann the elder upon the death of his wife, by whose bedside he had watched day and night. My grandfather, who had not seen him for a long time, hastened to join him at the Swanns' family property on the outskirts of Combray, and managed to entice him for a moment, weeping profusely, out of the death-chamber, so that he should not be present when the body was laid in its coffin. They took a turn or two in the park, where there was a little sunshine. Suddenly M. Swann seized my grandfather by the arm and cried, "Ah, my dear old friend, how fortunate we are to be walking here together on such a charming day! Don't you see how pretty they are, all these trees, my hawthorns, and my new pond, on which you have never congratulated me? You look as solemn as the grave. Don't you feel this little breeze? Ah! whatever you may say, it's good to be alive all the same, my dear Amédée!" And then, abruptly, the memory of his dead wife returned to him, and probably thinking it too complicated to inquire into how, at such a time, he could have allowed himself to be carried away by an impulse of happiness, he confined himself to a gesture which he habitually employed whenever any perplexing question came into his mind: that is, he passed his hand across his forehead, rubbed his eyes, and wiped his glasses. And yet he never got over the loss of his wife, but used to say to my grandfather, during the two years by which he survived her, "It's a funny thing, now; I very often think of my poor wife, but I cannot think of her for long at a time."

Translated from the French by C. K. Moncrieff
and Terence Kilmartin

Colette
1873–1954

Her Mother's Laughter

She was easily moved to laughter, a youthful, rather shrill laughter that brought tears to her eyes, and which she would afterwards deplore as inconsistent with the dignity of a mother burdened with the care of four children and financial worries. She would master her paroxysms of mirth, scolding herself severely, "Come, now, come! . . ." and then fall to laughing again till her pince-nez trembled on her nose.

We would jealously compete in our efforts to evoke her laughter, especially as we grew old enough to observe in her face, as the years succeeded each other, the ever-increasing shadow of anxiety for the morrow, a kind of distress which

sobered her whenever she thought of the fate of her penniless
children, or her precarious health, of old age that was slowing
the steps—a single leg and two crutches—of her beloved companion. When she was silent, my mother resembled all mothers
who are scared at the thought of poverty and death. But speech
brought back to her features an invincible youthfulness. Though
she might grow thin with sorrow, she never spoke sadly. She
would escape, as it were in one bound, from a painful reverie,
and pointing her knitting needle at her husband would exclaim:

"What? Just you try to die first, and you'll see!"

"I shall do my best, dear heart," he would answer.

She would glare at him as savagely as if he had carelessly
trodden on a pelargonium cutting or broken the little gold-
enamelled Chinese teapot.

"Isn't that just like you! You've got all the selfishness of
the Funels and the Colettes combined! Oh, why did I ever marry
you?"

"Because, my beloved, I threatened to blow out your brains
if you didn't."

"True enough. Even in those days, you see, you thought
only of yourself! And now here you are talking of nothing less
than of dying before me. All I say is, only let me see you try!"

He did try, and succeeded at the first attempt. He died in
his seventy-fourth year, holding the hands of his beloved, and
fixing on her weeping eyes a gaze that gradually lost its colour,
turned milky blue and faded like a sky veiled in mist. He was
given the handsomest of village funerals, a coffin of yellow
wood covered only by an old tunic riddled with wounds—the
tunic he had worn as a captain in the 1st Zouaves—and my
mother accompanied him steadily to the grave's edge, very small
and resolute beneath her widow's veil, and murmuring under
her breath words of love that only he must hear.

We brought her back to the house, and there she promptly
lost her temper with her new mourning, the cumbersome crape
that caught on the keys of doors and presses, the cashmere dress
that stifled her. She sat resting in the drawing-room near the big

green chair in which my father would never sit again and which the dog had already joyfully invaded. She was dry-eyed, flushed and feverish and kept on repeating:

"Oh, how hot it is! Heavens! The heat of this black stuff! Don't you think I might change now, into my blue sateen?"

"Well . . ."

"Why not? Because of my mourning? But I simply loathe black! For one thing, it's melancholy. Why should I present a sad and unpleasant sight to everyone I meet? What connection is there between this cashmere and crape and my feelings? Don't let me ever see you in mourning for me! You know well enough that I only like you to wear pink, and some shades of blue."

She got up hastily, took several steps towards an empty room and stopped abruptly:

"Ah! . . . Of course. . . ."

She came back and sat down again, admitting with a simple and humble gesture that she had, for the first time that day, forgotten that *he* was dead.

"Shall I get you something to drink, mother? Wouldn't you like to go to bed?"

"Of course not. Why should I? I'm not ill!"

She sat there and began to learn patience, staring at the floor, where a dusty track from the door of the sitting-room to the door of the empty bedroom had been marked by rough, heavy shoes.

A kitten came in, circumspect and trustful, a common and irresistible little kitten four or five months old. He was acting a dignified part for his own edification, pacing grandly, his tail erect as a candle, in imitation of lordly males. But a sudden and unexpected somersault landed him head over heels at our feet, where he took fright at his own temerity, rolled himself into a ball, stood up on his hind legs, danced sideways, arched his back, and then spun around like a top.

"Look at him, oh, do look at him, Minet-Chéri! Goodness! Isn't he funny!"

And she laughed, sitting there in her mourning, laughed her shrill, young girl's laugh, clapping her hands with delight at the kitten. Then, of a sudden, searing memory stemmed that brilliant cascade and dried the tears of laughter in my mother's eyes. Yet she offered no excuse for having laughed, either on that day, or on the days that followed; for though she had lost the man she passionately loved, in her kindness for us she remained among us just as she always had been, accepting her sorrow as she would have accepted the advent of a long and dreary season, but welcoming from every source the fleeting benediction of joy. So she lived on, swept by shadow and sunshine, bowed by bodily torments, resigned, unpredictable and generous, rich in children, flowers and animals like a fruitful domain.

Misunderstandings with the Living

If the grief of Colette's mother imposed no burden on those she loved, death often is an occasion that surfaces old resentments among family survivors and misunderstandings when individual members grieve in different ways. In the next selections, anthropologist Oscar Lewis records family disarray in the culture of Mexican poverty, novelist Anzia Yezierska speaks to a conflict between generations, and Shakespeare's Hamlet, literature's great and tormented mourner, castigates his mother for her unseemly haste in remarrying after the death of his father.

Oscar Lewis
1914–1970

Lewis' 1961 study of a poor Mexican family, *The Children of Sanchez*, was followed eight years later by *A Death in the Sanchez Family*, which focuses on a single dramatic incident, the death of the family's closest blood relative, Aunt Guadalupe, and their struggle to get her decently into the ground. For the poor, Lewis says, "death is almost as great a hardship as life itself." This selection is in the words of Guadalupe's niece Consuelo, who has returned to the village for the burial. Poverty underscores the anger and bitterness she feels toward other relatives.

Consuelo

At last the hearse and the funeral bus arrived. I felt my breast tighten. The hour of separation had come. When my aunt was carried out in my brothers' arms, I remembered her words, "I won't leave here until they carry me out feet first." How enormous a sadness I felt as I looked through the window of the hearse and saw her lying on her gray couch surrounded by flowers.

Matilde had brought alcohol and an onion in case I felt faint and Roberto stayed close to take care of me. His face, too, was wet with tears. Manuel glanced at me sideways, expecting me to give way to hysterical sobs, but I would not let him see me defeated. I carried myself proudly although my chest pained me and torment engulfed my throat.

We got into the bus and as we left I turned my face toward the *vecindad.* "Now, my little mother, you must leave forever. Here your house will stay. But don't worry, little one, I will take care of it." And so the funeral "procession" departed.

Unfortunately I had taken a seat behind Manuel and María and could hear their conversation. Manuel put his arm around his wife and they talked of business in the plaza. Not for a minute were their thoughts with us. Perhaps he was trying to distract me, because when we passed what had been the zone of the Nonoalco bridge he leaned forward and said to me, "The mayor has done some good here. As we go by take a look at the beautiful housing project he is putting up."

I scarcely turned my head to look, but rode along concentrating on my aunt, comforting and reassuring her. We passed by Avenida Melchor Campo, Avenida Gutenberg, Avenida Horacio where I once had friends and many illusions about my future. It was a world completely unknown to my aunt. She had never wanted to go out with me. All of them were a little afraid of me, because they say that I am severe and not like them. But I had loved her, and while we made that last trip I felt as if she were still watching over me, inviting me to go with her as she had when I was a child, turning her head to look for me, "And Skinny, where is she?"

"Here, dear one, I am here beside you." I felt that at any moment she would look around to see me. Scenes from her life passed through my mind.

I still hadn't seen her face, and I thought that when we arrived I would ask them to open the coffin. I had asked for holy water back at her house and someone had assured me that there would be water and a chapel where they could take the body and say a Mass. I had been looking forward to that. She should not go without some ceremony. So when we arrived we carried her coffin to the chapel where the priest, with a smile on his lips, invited us to enter. "Come in, come in. All who wish to may enter the house of God." But before giving the last rites he told us, "Thirty-five *pesos* for a Mass sung with the organ, twenty-five *pesos* for the ordinary Mass. You decide."

It offended me to see the disdainful way they commercialize and take advantage of these moments when grief keeps one from seeing clearly. Manuel, Roberto, Jaime, and I got together the money to pay for the Mass. I was glad to see Manuel make the move that most killed him, that is, to put his hand into his pocket and take out the money to pay his share.

The priest began to pray, and we knelt to join him. I bowed my head . . . the weight seemed so great that for a moment I thought I was going to fall, but Matilde held me by the shoulders. I raised my head and the faintness passed. My brother Roberto wept with bowed head. Matilde and Catarina did not cry; their daily lives are surrounded with grief and they have become immune. We sat down again, and I knew that the final moment was near. She would stay here, irrevocably alone. We would go back to resume our juggling on the tightrope of life.

The owner of the hearse charged us seventy-five *pesos*. It was more than we had agreed upon, but he said in this way he could give us a place that was not at the bottom of a gully. Manuel said that they take advantage of people at such times and I agreed. I was angry with my brother Roberto. My aunt had bought the right to a permanent plot in the cemetery and through his stupidity she was placed in another spot where she might be exhumed to make way for someone else. I continued to plead that she be buried with the rest of our family, but it wasn't possible.

At last I stood at the opening of the damp vault that was to receive her. I asked them to open the coffin. Manuel did not want to see her, but Roberto and I did. It comforted me to see her for the last time, her small face smooth yet with little furrows, wearing a faint expression of pain. Her eyes were beautiful, the lashes curled. I gazed on her with all my love, interring with her all the emotion that was within me. "Little mother . . . little mother . . ." I bit my lips.

They closed the coffin and began to lower it. I wanted to kiss it, but perhaps they thought I was going to throw myself in, because I felt hands holding me back.

As they finished filling the grave, I looked at the sky and at the surroundings. The place where she rested was lovely. She was at the foot of a large tree, like the *ahuehuete* tree she used to visit year after year on her pilgrimages to Chalma. There was greenery around her, and a little sun.

I asked God, Where do the poor find rest? Will they truly have rest? Tell me, oh God, what will happen after death to a life that has been lived in martyrdom? You have said, "Blessed are the poor, for theirs is the kingdom of heaven." But here they say, "We have to purify ourselves in the eternal fire." I rebel, oh Lord, not against Your holy purposes, but against what people say about the poor. I mourn Your life, oh Lord, told by a rosary of Your tears, by the blood of Your footsteps. But why, Lord, why this miserable death?

I knelt to smooth the earth over as if I were caressing her. One of my aunt's *comadres* found an evergreen sprig and put it on the grave, "so she will live forever." I arranged some flowers, her favorite ones, but that devil of a wife of Manuel's moved them back and mixed them with the rest. The horn began to honk impatiently. I climbed into the coach, and when the motor started something inside me was pulled apart. Through the rear window of the bus I could see her grave. She was alone and there she had to stay.

We came back. I fled to the emptiness of her room. Roberto

left, saying that he was tired. Manuel went back to the Casa Grande with María, saying, "In any case I am going to get something out of this. Think about it and we'll see." Matilde and Catarina returned to their little home. I stayed in my aunt's kitchen. Gaspar went into the bedroom and began to sob. Chocolate, the dog, scrambled to his feet. I wondered what would become of the dog and of my aunt's pigeons and cat. She and my uncle had always been fond of all their pets but Chocolate was their favorite. My aunt had treated him like her child and really, that dog did understand a lot. She would say to him, "Chocolate, come on in! You bark a lot, but when it gets right down to it you come around to lick my hand. You're all repentance, like that son of a bitch shrimp of a master of yours." And she would pick up her sandal and threaten him. When finally Chocolate came in and jumped into his box, she'd say, "Coward! You barked as if you meant business."

How I felt my aunt's absence! Gaspar came into the kitchen and after a while we began to talk. "Excuse me, *Señorita* Consuelo, what your brother said, that he would give me permission to stay here for only a few days . . . well, after all, it's for you to say, isn't it? It's no less than I could hope for."

"No, Gaspar, he has no right to tell you to go. Roberto did not know how to explain it well. You stay in the house. Matilde wants it too, but don't be upset. Tomorrow we'll see how to arrange things."

"Yes, but look, she has already started to take out some things. She took the glasses that were over there."

"Don't worry, Gaspar. She'll bring them back. And the brazier?"

"She took that too."

"I'll tell her to bring it back."

We spoke of my aunt, of the disputes they had had. He swore again and again that the stories were not true. I listened indifferently.

Matilde came over to invite me to eat with them. As we

entered the house, her father, José, arrived and shouted, "What happened? What do you want me for?"

I realized that they wanted to talk about my aunt's place. Well, at least they had shown a little tact in inviting me to sit down at their table. At any other time I would have refused, but this time I forgot my repugnance at eating there. I even forgot the odor from the toilets that Catarina never cleaned. I sat on the bed next to *Señor* José. To my left, on a board placed over a pail, Pancho sat with Matilde's young son beside him. Her daughter sat on the floor. Pancho turned a large pot upside down and used it as a table. Matilde was in the kitchen with her grandmother; Catarina served the food. They had prepared stewed chicken, the best food they had, for this day. They gave me hot chicken soup, bless them. It was something out of the ordinary in their lives. While she was serving, Catarina put bits of *taco* in her mouth and made jokes, trying to get me to forget. What affection I felt for them at that moment! The way in which one expresses concern for others may be insignificant, but the results are great.

Before they brought up the subject, I asked them, "It's about the house, isn't it? I understand that Matilde needs it. We don't have to decide right now, do we? There's plenty of time, and I'm so tired. Let's wait until tomorrow so we can go to our villas to rest and sun ourselves. We'll take a vacation first!" I made a sweeping gesture that made them all laugh.

The soup tasted delicious and the sauce that Matilde had made was also very good. I told her so and she replied like a child who has received a compliment, "*Ay yes . . . Ay*, no, it's very poor." I told her that it didn't taste just right because Gaspar hadn't eaten yet and I asked them to call him. He didn't want to come until I sent word that "I, *Señorita* Conseulo, say you are to come or I will go after you."

"Oh," said Catarina, "Roberto told him that he wasn't to touch a drop of wine."

"Yes, but I told Roberto that life is sacred, and we have no right to interfere in Gaspar's."

"But if he drinks he might become indecent, as he did at the wake," said Matilde.

"Look, don't pay any attention to him. Just let him talk," I told her. "This happens to everyone when they drink. The same thing has happened to you, yes, even to my aunt when they were passing the bottle around."

Gaspar came in. "You sent for me, *Señorita* Consuelo?"

"Sit down, Gaspar, and have something to eat."

"Maybe he doesn't want to," said Catarina. "I've invited him many times before and he didn't come."

When the meal was over I asked Matilde to return the brazier and the glasses and told Catarina to look after the house. I implored them to recite a rosary and then to eat docilely.

"But now you want to, don't you, Gaspar?" He began. I said good-bye, leaving by the path in the courtyard where I had so often come in search of peace or comfort for my soul.

I went to spend the night at my half-sister Antonia's house. On my last trip to Mexico City I had brought from the north some new clothing that I wanted to sell. I left some dresses with Antonia and promised to give her a commission if she sold them. I did the same with my sister Marta but she took the clothing back to Acapulco with her and I hadn't heard from her since. I hoped that Antonia had some money for me. I needed it so badly!

Antonia and her husband were surprised to see me. "Why didn't you let us know you were coming?"

"There wasn't time. I have just come from my aunt's funeral."

"And why didn't anyone let us know?"

"I don't know. I just arrived this morning."

They were playing popular music on the record player, with the volume turned up high. Antonia wore a new gold dressing gown which surprised me because fifteen days before she didn't have enough money to buy a comb and I had left her mine. We had a drink and then my brother-in-law left to go after a dress he had bought his daughter for her birthday party the next day. With some misgivings, I asked Antonia about the money for the clothes. "What happened, Tonia? Did you sell the things?"

"Yes, Consuelo, but can you believe it? They haven't paid me yet."

I didn't say anything but I knew what had happened. She had bought clothes for herself and her daughter and only God knew if I would ever get my money. I kept silent and asked her little girl to join me in saying a rosary before we went to bed. "You'd better hurry and say your prayers before my husband gets back," Antonia said. "You know he doesn't like these things." We were still praying when he came in, but he respected our feelings and didn't protest.

The following day, with the little money I had left, I paid my aunt's landlord part of the four month's rent she owed him. He agreed to wait for the rest. Then I went back to the *vecindad* and at last convinced Gaspar and Matilde to share my aunt's place. I told Matilde she could move in on condition that she would take care of everything as if my aunt were still there. To honor her memory, the altar and the religious pictures especially were to remain as they were. Whether they meant it or not, Matilde and Gaspar agreed. Then I went through my aunt's possessions, and divided them up between the two of them and a few friendly neighbors. For myself I kept the shawl I had sent my aunt money for. It was her pride, Gaspar told me. I also took her papers, her scissors, and two figures of the *Niño Dios*, and I got back the iron she had pawned. I didn't want to see anyone else use the clothes she wore the most, so I burned them. Then I gave some money to the woman who had helped her, five *pesos* to Gaspar, one to Matilde for her child's milk, and one to my godchild. I gave them my address and left, promising to return. It was late and again I slept at Antonia's.

The next morning I bought my return ticket to Nuevo Laredo and went to Manuel's house to get his signature giving permission for his children to leave the country. He was eating breakfast. Roberto was sitting on a bench outside waiting for him. By lying a little, I had no trouble getting Manuel to sign the papers. He didn't care enough about the children to even ask any questions. Before I left, I gave Roberto ten *pesos*.

All that day I walked alone. In the afternoon I looked for a church, went into a *café*, and finally left on the bus, carrying with me more grief and sorrow than I had ever borne before, my body in tatters and my whole life a moan.

Anzia Yezierska
1885–1970

Yezierska was well known in the 1920s for her realistic stories of Jewish immigrant life on New York's Lower East Side. Her autobiographical novel, *Bread Givers*, is subtitled "A struggle between a father of the Old World and a daughter of the New." This selection follows the death of the overworked mother of the young schoolteacher who has been trying to break away from the patriarchy of her father and his religion. During her mother's illness, her father had been taking his supper upstairs with the Widow Feinstein, who has her eye not only on him but on the Lodge money he will inherit.

Death in Hester Street

When I came back to my senses, the house was crowded. I found myself on the lounge, Bessie putting cold towels over my head. Mashah and Fania were tearing their hair and shrieking hysterically, "Mamma—Mamma!" For the first time in my life I saw Father weeping, like a lost child. Never before did I see him suffer. How strange he looked! His old veined hand holding a red kerchief, hiding his face, his gray beard trembling, his whole body bent and shaken with sobs. For the first time I realized

that he was old and that he was without Mother. Rushing over
to him I flung my arms around his neck, and wept with him.

People coming and going. Wailing and screaming. Tumult
and confusion. I saw Mother laid out in her coffin. The eyes that
but a few hours before filled me with light, those eyes were
tightly shut, sunken deep in their sockets. The nose drawn in,
bluish pallor staining the nostrils. Lower jaw dropped, revealing
stubs of decayed teeth. Ears yellow as wax. This was death. This
was not Mother. I stared and stared, and I felt myself turning to
ice, staring.

I touched the sunken lids where the eyes had shone on me
with such ineffable love. My hand withdrew, shuddering. Cold,
icy Death. Mother no more.

Where? Where has it gone, that light, that spark, that
love that looked into mine? What has it to do with that cold
clay? It's here, here, here in my heart. She's in me, around me.
Nothing in that clay.

I felt a hand under my arm leading me away into the
kitchen. In one heart-breaking monotone Father wailed:

"Woe! Woe! My house is fallen! My burden bearer gone!
Who'll take care of me now? Who'll cook me my meals? Who'll
wash me my clothes? Who'll light me my Sabbath candles?
For forty years I protected you, watched over you, prayed for
you. Now you're torn away from me. Be a good messenger to
God for me. Beg him not to forsake me. Not leave me in loneliness. O God! God! Help me in my woe! Give me strength to
stand my loss."

As Father crumpled into a heap, spent with grief, the
widow Mrs. Feinstein began to howl at the top of her voice,
wringing her hands and rocking herself over the coffin. "My best
friend! My neighbour! Forgive me if I talked evil of you. I take
it all back. I didn't mean nothing. Who would know that you
would die so soon? Forgive me. Be a good messenger to God
for me. Pray in Heaven for me. Beg God to be merciful to me
and spare me all ills."

Other neighbours came in screaming, tearing their hair,

and beating their breasts. Falling on the coffin and begging the dead body to forgive their evil talk during her lifetime. Begging the corpse to be a messenger in Heaven for them, to beg God to spare them all ills.

The room become crowded with all kinds of old and middle-aged men and women. Some moaning with grief, others with stony, serious faces. In the eyes of the old, fear of their own end.

A chorus of wailing neighbours gathered about the body, rocking and swaying and wringing their hands in woe.

"Such a good mother, such a virtuous wife," wailed a shawled woman with a nursing baby in her arms and two little tots hanging to her skirts. "Never did she allow herself a bite to eat but left-overs, never a dress but the rags her daughters had thrown away."

"Such a cook! Such a housewife!" groaned a white-haired old woman wiping her eyes with a corner of her shawl. "Only two days ago she told me how they cook the fish in her village sweet and sour—and now, she is dead."

At this, all the women began rocking and swaying in a wailing chorus.

"Only a week ago she was telling me she was getting better," began the widow Mrs. Feinstein. "But I saw it was her end."

"Yesterday morning, she was telling me if she'll only get well, she'll stop worrying and take it easy. And now . . ."

Floods of tears were shed by these strangers, but my eyes were dry. My heart was numb. My mind became a petrified blank. Suddenly I heard the undertaker, cold and unconcerned, announce:

"Members of the family take your last look!"

We filed around the coffin, frozen with grief.

The lid shut down. A shriek from the whole crowded room burst through the air as the undertaker ground the screws into the coffin. "Never shall we see her face again. Never, never!" it echoed and re-echoed. "Never shall we see her face again. Never."

The undertaker, with a knife in his hand, cut into Father's

coat and he rent his garments according to the Biblical law and ages of tradition. Then he slit my sisters' waists, and they, too, did as Father had done. Then the man turned to me with the knife in his hand. "No," I cried. "I feel terrible enough without tearing my clothes."

"It has to be done."

"I don't believe in this. It's my only suit, and I need it for work. Tearing it wouldn't bring Mother back to life again."

A hundred eyes burned on me their condemnation.

"Look at her, the *Americanerin!*"

"Heart of stone."

"A lot she cares for her mother's death."

"Not a tear did she shed. Her face is washed. Her hair is combed. Did we care how we looked when our mothers died?"

Four shabby-looking, frail, ill-fed poor men lifted the coffin on their shoulders. People pushed back on both sides to make room for the men to pass. Louder shrieks burst through the air again as the coffin was borne out of the house, through the crowded hall, and down the crowded stoop. Passers-by joined in the hysterical shrieks. They didn't know who died, but were drawn in by the common grief of death.

The coffin was pushed into the hearse. The door shut with a bang.

We stood jammed in by neighbours, waiting for the carriage to take us to the cemetery. All I saw were mobs and mobs of strangers staring at us. And all I heard was the clanking of coins in tin boxes, and insistent begging voices, exhorting the people, "Charity saves you from death! Charity saves you from death!"

LODGE MONEY

I had failed to give Mother the understanding of her deeper self during her lifetime. Let me at least give it to Father while he was yet alive. And so, every day, after school, I went to see him.

He did not look so forlorn as I thought he would. He

looked like one who had straightened out his back after the strain of a long, heavy burden. Perhaps he was glad that Mother's sufferings were over. Then I noticed he began wearing his Sabbath clothes for every day. He began to polish his shoes and comb his beard like for a holiday. Once I found him gazing at himself in the mirror and smiling with an innocent joyfulness that made me wonder how he could be so childishly happy when Mother was dead. He still ate his meals upstairs at Mrs. Feinstein's. But before, he used to eat there only his suppers. Now, he ate there three times a day.

Often I wanted to ask him if he was getting his food cooked just right, but I hated to speak of that widow. The mere thought of that woman filled me with a blind dislike that I couldn't reason about.

One day, I came and found her sewing a button on Father's shirt. After a hasty greeting she walked out. She must have known how I felt toward her.

As the door closed behind her, Father exclaimed, "What a womanly woman! What a virtuous soul! All she thinks of is how to cook for me the things I like and how to please me the most. The more I see her, the more I feel what a diamond treasure she is. How she could make a man happy!"

I stared at Father. What had happened to him! Was he bereft of his senses? That such a spiritual man could find anything in that bold-faced barrel of fat!

"In my misfortune, God yet sent me a great good luck," Father went on. "She's so kind, so nice to me. God punished me with one hand and blessed me with the other."

I looked at Father's guileless face and longed to shake him out of his blind foolishness, tell him about the world, about scheming women. But I was too angry to speak. My lips tightened, struggling to control myself.

"You ought to taste her *kugel*, her *gefülte* fish! Her cooking puts a new taste in life. And she's so quick and handy. Her table is set with a clean tablecloth for every day. And the knives and forks and even a paper napkin is all laid out, waiting for me, when I come. Every time I see her, her face is washed, her hair is combed and a clean apron. Always there's a smile on her face. The sun shines from her. I can see she's a woman who don't curse like other women."

I shuddered, as he went on, exulting in that woman's virtues. After Mother's devotion, how could he turn to such a creature? The thought of her sitting in Mother's chair, occupying Mother's bed, revolted me.

A few days after, when I called, I noticed Father avoided my eyes. He walked up and down, awkward and uncomfortable, as if he had something on his mind that bothered him. Suddenly, he stopped pacing the floor, brought his chair in front of me, and sat down.

"I have something to tell you," he began. "You understand a little more than your sisters, because you have a little bit of my head on you."

He paused and again avoided my eyes. I felt something terrible coming. I waited, my heart pounding in my throat.

"You know I can't remain alone. And I can't live with any of you children, because none of you are religious enough. I have to have my own house and someone to take care of me. It says in the Torah, a man must have a wife to keep himself pure, otherwise his eyes are tempted by evil. It says no man needs to wait more than thirty days after his wife's death to marry again. And I couldn't find a better woman than Mrs. Feinstein."

The room began to rock. Everything whirled before me in a blur.

Thirty days! Mother not yet cold in her grave. And he already planning for a new wife!

William Shakespeare
1564–1616

from *Hamlet*

Hamlet: O, that this too too sullied flesh would melt,
Thaw and resolve itself into a dew!
Or that the Everlasting had not fix'd
His canon 'gainst self-slaughter! O God! God!
How weary, stale, flat and unprofitable,
Seem to me all the uses of this world!
Fie on't! ah fie! 'tis an unweeded garden,
That grows to seed; things rank and gross in nature
Possess it merely. That it should come to this!
But two months dead; nay, not so much, not two:
So excellent a king; that was, to this,
Hyperion to a satyr; so loving to my mother
That he might not beteem the winds of heaven
Visit her face too roughly. Heaven and earth!
Must I remember? Why, she would hang on him,
As if increase of appetite had grown
By what it fed on: and yet, within a month—
Let me not think on't—Frailty, thy name is woman!—
A little month, or ere those shoes were old
With which she follow'd my poor father's body,
Like Niobe, all tears:—why she, even she—
O God! a beast, that wants discourse of reason,
Would have mourn'd longer—married with my uncle,
My father's brother, but no more like my father
Than I to Hercules: within a month:
Ere yet the salt of most unrighteous tears
Had left the flushing in her galled eyes,
She married. O, most wicked speed, to post
With such dexterity to incestuous sheets!
It is not nor it cannot come to good:
But break, my heart; for I must hold my tongue.

Act I, Scene 2

Mourning the Loss of a Child

The death of a child seems a violation of the natural order and may be the hardest grief to absorb and work through. For the parents in the next selections, the act of writing provides a way of keeping the child alive, even in the poor substitute of words. The poems by Stan Rice and Robert Frost and the story by Maeve Brennan offer insight into the conflicts between mothers and fathers as they grieve in their individual ways. And Charles Lamb, John Crowe Ransom and Theodore Roethke remind us that those outside the family need to express their grief when a child dies.

Joseph von Eichendorff
1788–1857

On My Child's Death

Clocks strike in the distance,
Already the night grows late,
How dimly the lamp glistens;
Your bed is all made.

It is the wind goes, only,
Grieving around the house;
Where, inside, we sit lonely
Often listening out.

It is as if, how lightly,
You must be going to knock,

Had missed your way and might be
Tired, no, coming back.

We are poor, poor stupid folk!
It's we, still lost in dread,
Who wander in the dark—
You've long since found your bed.

Translated from the German by W. D. Snodgrass

Po Chü-i
772–846

P'u—Hua Fei Hua

A flower and not a flower; of mist yet not of mist;
At midnight she was there; she went as daylight shone.
She came and for a little while was like a dream of spring,
And then, as morning clouds that vanish traceless, she was gone.

Translated from the Chinese by Duncan Mackintosh;
rendered into verse by Alan Ayling

Ben Jonson
1573–1637

On My First Son

Farewell, thou child of my right hand, and joy!
   My sinne was too much hope of thee, lov'd boy,
Seven yeeres thou wert lent to me, and I thee pay,
   Exacted by thy fate, on the just day.

O, could I lose all Father, now. For why
    Will man lament the state he should envie?
To have so soone scap'd world's, and flesh's rage,
    And, if no other miserie, yet age?

Rest in soft peace, and, ask'd, say here doth lye
    Ben Jonson his best piece of poetrie:
For whose sake, henceforth, all his vowes be such,
    As what he loves may never like too much.

Sir John Beaumont
1583–1627

Of My Dear Son Gervaise

Can I, who have for others oft compil'd
The songs of death, forget my sweetest child,
Which, like a flow'r crush'd, with a blast is dead,
And ere full time hands down his smiling head,
Expecting with clear hope to live anew,
Among the angels fed with heav'nly dew? . . .
Dear Lord, receive my son, whose winning love
To me was like a friendship, far above
The course of nature or his tender age;
Whose looks could all my bitter griefs assuage:
Let his pure soul, ordain'd seven years to be
In that frail body which was part of me,
Remain my pledge in Heav'n, as sent to show
How to this port at every step I go.

Paiute Indian Song

Lament of a Man for His Son

Son, my son!
   I will go up to the mountain
And there I will light a fire
To the feet of my own son's spirit,
And there will I lament him;
Saying,
O my son,
What is my life to me, now you are departed?

Son, my son,
In the deep earth
We softly laid thee
In a chief's robe,
In a warrior's gear.
Surely there,
In the spirit land
Thy deeds attend thee!
Surely,
The corn comes to the ear again!
But I, here,
I am the stalk that the seed-gatherers
Descrying empty, afar, left standing.
Son, my son!
What is my life to me, now you are departed?

Denise Jallais

An editor of *Elle* magazine, Jallais lives in Geneva.

Lullaby for My Dead Child
You shouldn't be afraid of the dark
Or of worms
Besides
Now you can play with the rain
And see the grass come up

You shouldn't put dirt in your mouth
And sit still waiting for me
Besides
We've given you some flowers
To console you for being little
And dead.

Translated by Maxine Kumin and Judith Kumin

Frances Gunther

John Gunther, Jr., son of the American journalist and Frances Gunther, died in 1947 at the age of seventeen. Johnny was a particularly bright and engaging young man; he corresponded with Albert Einstein and looked forward to entering Harvard University. His father documented his brave battle with illness in the 1949 memoir *Death Be Not Proud*. The memoir concludes with Johnny's mother's response to his death. Her words suggest that for a parent who survives a child, there are regrets beyond reason or solace.

from *Death Be Not Proud*

My grief, I find, is not desolation or rebellion at universal law or deity. I find grief to be much simpler and sadder. Contemplating the Eternal Deity and His Universal Laws leaves me grave but dry-eyed. But a sunny fast wind along the Sound, good sailing weather, a new light boat, will shame me to tears: how Johnny would have loved this boat, this wind, this sunny day! . . .

Missing him now, I am haunted by my own shortcomings, how often I failed him. I think every parent must have a sense of failure, even of sin, merely in remaining alive after the death of a child. One feels that it is not right to live when one's child has died, that one should somehow have found the way to give one's life to save his life. Failing there, one's failures during his too brief life seem all the harder to bear and forgive. How often I wish I had not sent him away to school when he was still so young that he wanted to remain at home in his own room, with his own things and his own parents. How I wish we had maintained the marriage that created the home he loved so much. How I wish we had been able before he died to fulfill his last heart's desires: the talk with Professor Einstein, the visit to Harvard Yard, the dance with his friend Mary.

These desires seem so simple. How wonderful they would have been to him. All the wonderful things in life are so simple that one is not aware of their wonder until they are beyond touch. Never have I felt the wonder and beauty and joy of life so keenly as now in my grief that Johnny is not here to enjoy them.

Today, when I see parents impatient or tired or bored with their children, I wish I could say to them, But they are alive, think of the wonder of that! They may be a care and a burden, but think, they are alive! You can touch them—what a miracle! You don't have to hold back sudden tears when you see just a headline about the Yale-Harvard game because you know your boy will never see the Yale-Harvard game, never see the house in Paris he was born in, never bring home his girl, and you will not hand down your jewels to his bride and will have no grandchildren to play with and spoil. Your sons and daughters are alive. Think of that—not dead but alive! Exult and sing.

All parents who have lost a child will feel what I mean. Others, luckily, cannot. But I hope they will embrace them with a little added rapture and a keener awareness of joy.

I wish we had loved Johnny more when he was alive. Of course we loved Johnny very much. Johnny knew that. Everybody knew it. Loving Johnny more. What does it mean? What can it mean, now?

Parents all over the earth who lost sons in the war have felt this kind of question, and sought an answer. To me, it means loving life more, being more aware of life, of one's fellow human beings, of the earth.

It means obliterating, in a curious but real way, the ideas of evil and hate and the enemy, and transmuting them, with the alchemy of suffering, into ideas of clarity and charity.

It means caring more and more about other people, at home and abroad, all over the earth. It means caring more about God.

I hope we can love Johnny more and more till we too die, and leave behind us, as he did, the love of love, the love of life.

Lolly Quinones
1934–1979

February

Month of great men
And for us, a family month
Of birthdays, both grandfathers,
And one son.

In California, it's
The month of flowering fruit—
Glory of white-blossomed pears,
The dazzling peach in pinks and reds,
Pale Oriental plum.

Now, suddenly,
A month of death.
Trees bloom
But not our second-born son.

Stopped, his turning
Growth in time.
Forever now eighteen,
Forever muscled,
Mustached, moving
In our remembering minds.
Forever budding, burgeoning
His art, his thought, his life,
Never to unfold in flower
Or reach the summertime of fruit.

Our month of birthdays
Sombered and subdued;
He died
And fruit trees all over town
Burst into spring.

Ralph Waldo Emerson
1803–1882

In a long poem written after the death of his young son in 1847,
Emerson's belief in the divinity of the individual feeds the im-

pulse to sanctify the dead that so often accompanies mourning. The child he describes has been divested of any homely, human traits. The father's anger at the death is directed at nature and a world not yet ready to understand such perfection of being.

---

from *Threnody*

Was there no star that could be sent,
No watcher in the firmament,
No angel from the countless host
That loiters round the crystal coast,
Could stoop to heal that only child,
Nature's sweet marvel undefiled,
And keep the blossom of the earth,
Which all her harvests were not worth?
Not mine, —I never called thee mine,
But Nature's heir,—if I repine,
And seeing rashly torn and moved
Not what I made, but what I loved,
Grow early old with grief that thou
Must to the wastes of Nature go,—
'Tis because a general hope was quenched, and all must doubt
      and grope.
For flattering planets seemed to say
This child should ills of ages stay,
By wondrous tongue, and guided pen,
Bring the flown Muses back to men.
Perchance not he but Nature ailed,
The world and not the infant failed.
It was not ripe yet to sustain
A genius of so fine a strain,
Who gazed upon the sun and moon
As if he came unto his own,
And, pregnant with his grander thought,
Brought the old order into doubt.

His beauty once their beauty tried;
They could not feed him, and he died,
And wandered backward as in scorn,
To wait an aeon to be born. . . .

The eager fate which carried thee
Took the largest part of me:
For this losing is true dying;
This is lordly man's down-lying,
This his slow but sure reclining,
Star by star his world resigning.

Stan Rice

In a struggle between parents for possession of the dead child, the father here addresses the mother, the illustrious one, in an effort to save his sanity against the excesses of her vagrant grief.

Singing Death

Illustrious one, in whom death is the vagrom wound
& who wanders on the wet grasses singing, sing no more
to me. I have heard your voice plenty & I hunger for health.
Yes, though it is beautiful & seduces, Hush. Come no more
glaze-eyed to my arms asking for pity then push me aside
when the urge strikes to start singing. Transfixed
& then unhinged, crazed with the wish to die & then with the fear
the wish might be granted. I have heard your song
and it shall not drag me yet down with it on the wet grasses.

Illustrious one, in whom death goes on living season by season,
drawing its strength from your singing, lovely
& deadly, Listen: I will not make myself

dead to nourish the death
blooming within you, vagrom intensity. Rather than that I'd see
you wandering lost on the white watery lawns at midnight
singing for the police to come get you, yes, even rather
see you staring at a white wall trying to sing the shapes
out of the whiteness than continue this dying together.

Illustrious one, in whom death is no longer a solid block
but a network, sing no more to me of the waterglass & the
    stopped clock.
Against such songs we've crashed enough, enough.
That which was from the heart and was heart's song
has been transformed, a heartless net in which to sing
is to struggle and suffer humiliation at the hour of death.
You who sing out of the vagrom flower-mouth-wound, go back!
The white grasses will release you, bones & voice & dress
one entity, dignity regained, deathsong left where you leave
your shape on the lawn in the wet blades. Singing yet.

Robert Frost
1874–1963

Home Burial

He saw her from the bottom of the stairs
Before she saw him. She was starting down,
Looking back over her shoulder at some fear.
She took a doubtful step and then undid it
To raise herself and look again. He spoke
Advancing toward her: "What is it you see
From up there always—for I want to know."
She turned and sank upon her skirts at that,
And her face changed from terrified to dull.
He said to gain time: "What is it you see,"

Mounting until she cowered under him.
"I will find out now—you must tell me, dear."
She, in her place, refused him any help
With the least stiffening of her neck and silence
She let him look, sure that he wouldn't see,
Blind creature; and a while he didn't see.
But at last he murmured, "Oh," and again, "Oh."

"What is it—what?" she said.

                                        "Just that I see."

"You don't," she challenged. "Tell me what it is."

"The wonder is I didn't see at once.
I never noticed it from here before.
I must be wonted to it—that's the reason.
The little graveyard where my people are!
So small the window frames the whole of it.
Not so much larger than a bedroom, is it?
There are three stones of slate and one of marble,
Broad-shouldered little slabs there in the sunlight
On the sidehill. We haven't to mind *those*.
But I understand: it is not the stones,
But the child's mound—"

                        "Don't, don't, don't, don't," she cried.

She withdrew shrinking from beneath his arm
That rested on the banister, and slid downstairs;
And turned on him with such a daunting look,
He said twice over before he knew himself:
"Can't a man speak of his own child he's lost?"

"Not you! Oh, where's my hat? Oh, I don't need it!
I must get out of here. I must get air.
I don't know rightly whether any man can."

"Amy! Don't go to someone else this time.
Listen to me. I won't come down the stairs."
He sat and fixed his chin between his fists.
"There's something I should like to ask you, dear."

"You don't know how to ask it."

                                        "Help me, then."

Her fingers moved the latch for all reply.

"My words are nearly always an offence.
I don't know how to speak of anything
So as to please you. But I might be taught
I should suppose. I can't say I see how.
A man must partly give up being a man
With women-folk. We could have some arrangement
By which I'd bind myself to keep hands off
Anything special you're a-mind to name.
Though I don't like such things 'twixt those that love.
Two that don't love can't live together without them.
But two that do can't live together with them."
She moved the latch a little. "Don't—don't go.
Don't carry it to someone else this time.
Tell me about it if it's something human.
Let me into your grief. I'm not so much
Unlike other folks as your standing there
Apart would make me out. Give me my chance.
I do think, though, you overdo it a little.
What was it brought you up to think it the thing
To take your mother-loss of a first child
So inconsolably—in the face of love.
You'd think his memory might be satisfied—"

"There you go sneering now!"

                                        "I'm not, I'm not!"

You make me angry. I'll come down to you.
God, what a woman! And it's come to this,
A man can't speak of his own child that's dead."

"You can't because you don't know how to speak.
If you had any feelings, you that dug
With your own hand—how could you?—his little grave;
I saw you from that very window there,
Making the gravel leap and leap in air,
Leap up, like that, like that, and land so lightly
And roll back down the mound beside the hole.
I thought, Who is that man? I didn't know you.
And I crept down the stairs and up the stairs
To look again, and still your spade kept lifting.
Then you came in. I heard your rumbling voice
Out in the kitchen, and I don't know why,
But I went near to see with my own eyes.
You could sit there with the stains on your shoes
Of the fresh earth from your own baby's grave
And talk about your everyday concerns.
You had stood the spade up against the wall
Outside there in the entry, for I saw it."

"I shall laugh the worst laugh I ever laughed.
I'm cursed. God, if I don't believe I'm cursed."

"I can repeat the very words you were saying.
'Three foggy mornings and one rainy day
Will rot the best birch fence a man can build.'
Think of it, talk like that at such a time!
What had how long it takes a birch to rot
To do with what was in the darkened parlour.
You *couldn't* care! The nearest friends can go
With anyone to death, comes so far short
They might as well not try to go at all.
No, from the time when one is sick to death,

One is alone, and he dies more alone.
Friends make pretence of following to the grave,
But before one is in it, their minds are turned
And making the best of their way back to life
And living people, and things they understand.
But the world's evil. I won't have grief so
If I can change it. Oh, I won't, I won't!"

"There, you have said it all and you feel better.
You won't go now. You're crying. Close the door.
The heart's gone out of it: why keep it up.
Amy! There's someone coming down the road!"

"*You*—oh, you think the talk is all. I must go—
Somewhere out of this house. How can I make you—"

"If—you—do!" She was opening the door wider.
"Where do you mean to go? First tell me that.
I'll follow and bring you back by force. I *will!*—"

Maeve Brennan

The Eldest Child

Mrs. Bagot had lived in the house for fifteen years, ever since her marriage. Her three children had been born there, in the upstairs front bedroom, and she was glad of that, because her first child, her son, was dead, and it comforted her to think that she was still familiar with what had been his one glimpse of earth— he had died at three days. At the time he died she said to herself that she would never get used to it, and what she meant by that was that as long as she lived she would never accept what had happened in the mechanical subdued way that the rest of them accepted it. They carried on, they talked and moved about her room as though when they tidied the baby away they had really tidied him away, and it seemed to her that more than anything else they expressed the hope that nothing more would be said about him. They behaved as though what had happened was finished, as though some ordinary event had taken place and come to an end in a natural way. There had not been an ordinary event, and it had not come to an end.

Lying in her bed, Mrs. Bagot thought her husband and the rest of them seemed very strange, or else, she thought fearfully, perhaps it was she herself who was strange, delirious, or even a bit unbalanced. If she was unbalanced she wasn't going to let them know about it—not even Martin, who kept looking at her with frightened eyes and telling her she must try to rest. It might be better not to talk, yet she was very anxious to explain how she felt. Words did no good. Either they did not want to hear her, or they were not able to hear her. What she was trying to tell them seemed very simple to her. What had happened could not come to an end, that was all. It could not come to an end. Without a memory, how was the baby going to find his way? Mrs. Bagot would have liked to ask that question, but she wanted to express it properly, and she thought if she could just be left alone for a while she would be able to find the right words, so that she could make herself clearly understood—but they wouldn't leave her alone. They kept trying to rouse her, and yet when she spoke for any length of time they always silenced her by telling her it was God's will. She had accepted God's will all her life without argument, and she was not arguing now, but she knew that what had happened was not finished, and she was sure it was not God's will that she be left in this bewilderment. All she wanted was to say how she felt, but they mentioned God's will as though they were slamming a door between her and some territory that was forbidden to her. But only to her; everybody else knew all about it. She alone must lie quiet and silent under this semblance of ignorance that they wrapped about her like a shroud. They wanted her to be silent and not speak of this knowledge she had now, the knowledge that made her afraid. It was the same knowl-

edge they all had, of course, but they did not want it spoken of.
Everything about her seemed false, and Mrs. Bagot was tired of
everything. She was tired of being told that she must do this for
her own good and that she must do that for her own good, and
it annoyed her when they said she was being brave—she was
being what she had to be, she had no alternative. She felt very
uncomfortable and out of place, and as though she had failed, but
she did not know whether to push her failure away or comfort
it, and in any case it seemed to have drifted out of reach.

She was not making sense. She could not get her thoughts
sorted out. Something was drifting away—that was as far as she
could go in her mind. No wonder she couldn't talk properly.
What she wanted to say was really quite simple. Two things.
First, there was the failure that had emptied and darkened her
mind until nothing remained now but a black wash. Second,
there was something that drifted and dwindled, always dwindling,
until it was now no more than a small shape, very small, not to
be identified except as something lost. Mrs. Bagot thought she
was the only one who could still identify that shape, and she was
afraid to take her eyes off it, because it became constantly smaller,
showing as it diminished the new horizons it was reaching, although it drifted so gently it seemed not to move at all. Mrs.
Bagot would never have dreamed her mind could stretch so far,
or that her thoughts could follow so faithfully, or that she could
watch so steadily, without tears or sleep.

The fierce demands that had been made on her body and on
her attention were finished. She could have met all those demands, and more. She could have moved mountains. She had
found that the more the child demanded of her, the more she
had to give. Her strength came up in waves that had their source
in a sea of calm and unconquerable devotion. The child's holy
trust made her open her eyes, and she took stock of herself and
found that everything was all right, and that she could meet what
challenges arose and meet them well, and that she had nothing
to apologize for—on the contrary, she had every reason to rejoice. Her days took on an orderliness that introduced her to a

sense of ease and confidence she had never been told about. The house became a kingdom, significant, private, and safe. She smiled often, a smile of innocent importance.

Perhaps she had let herself get too proud. She had seen at once that the child was unique. She had been thankful, but perhaps not thankful enough. The first minute she had held him in her arms, immediately after he was born, she had seen his friendliness. He was fine. There was nothing in the world the matter with him. She had remarked to herself that his tiny face had a very humorous expression, as though he already knew exactly what was going on. And he was determined to live. He was full of fight. She had felt him fight toward life with all her strength, and then again, with all her strength. In a little while, he would have recognized her.

What she watched now made no demands on anyone. There was no impatience there, and no impatience in her, either. She lay on her side, and her hand beat gently on the pillow in obedience to words, an old tune, that had been sounding in her head for some time, and that she now began to listen to. It was an old song, very slow, a tenor voice from long ago and far away. She listened idly.

> "Oft in the stilly night
> Ere slumber's chain hath bound me
> Fond memory brings the light
> Of other days around me."

Over and over and over again, the same words, the same kind, simple words. Mrs. Bagot thought she must have heard that song a hundred times or more.

> "Oft in the stilly night
> Ere slumber's chain hath bound me
> Fond memory brings the light
> Of other days around me.
> The smiles, the tears, of boyhood's years

The words of love then spoken
The eyes that shone, now dimmed and gone
The cheerful hearts now broken."

It was a very kind song. She had never noticed the words before, even though she knew them well. Loving words, loving eyes, loving hearts. The faraway voice she listened to was joined by others, as the first bird of dawn is joined by other birds, all telling the same story, telling it over and over again, because it is the only story they know.

There was the song, and then, there was the small shape that drifted uncomplainingly from distant horizon to still more distant horizon. Mrs. Bagot closed her eyes. She felt herself being beckoned to a place where she could hide, for the time being.

For the past day or so, she had turned from everyone, even from Martin. He no longer attempted to touch her. He had not even touched her hand since the evening he knelt down beside the bed and tried to put his arms around her. She struggled so fiercely against him that he had to let her go, and he stood up and stepped away from her. It really seemed she might injure herself, fighting against him, and that she would rather injure herself than lie quietly against him, even for a minute. He could not understand her. It was his loss as much as hers, but she behaved as though it had to do only with her. She pushed him away, and then when she was free of him she turned her face away from him and began crying in a way that pleaded for attention and consolation from someone, but not from him—that was plain. But before that, when she was pushing him away, he had seen her face, and the expression on it was of hatred. She might have been a wild animal, for all the control he had over her then, but if so she was a wild animal in a trap, because she was too weak to go very far. He pitied her, and the thought sped through his mind that if she could get up and run, or fly, he would let her go as far as she wished, and hope she would come back to him in her own time, when her anger and grief were spent. But he forgot that thought immediately in his panic at her distress, and he called down to the woman who had come in to help around the house, and asked her to come up at once. She had heard the noise and was on her way up anyway, and she was in the room almost as soon as he called—Mrs. Knox, a small, red-faced, gray-haired woman who enjoyed the illusion that life had nothing to teach her.

"Oh, I've been afraid of this all day," she said confidently, and she began to lift Mrs. Bagot up so that she could straighten the pillows and prop her up for her tea. But Mrs. Bagot struck out at the woman and began crying, "Oh, leave me alone, leave me alone. Why can't the two of you leave me alone." Then she wailed, "Oh, leave me alone," in a high strange voice, an artificial voice, and at that moment Mr. Bagot became convinced that she was acting, and that the best thing to do was walk off and leave her there, whether that was what she really wanted or not. Oh, but he loved her. He stared at her, and said to himself that it would have given him the greatest joy to see her lying there with the baby in her arms, but although that was true, the reverse was not true—to see her lying there as she was did not cause him terrible grief or anything like it. He felt ashamed and lonely and impatient, and he longed to say to her, "Delia, stop all this nonsense and let me talk to you." He wanted to appear masterful and kind and understanding, but she drowned him out with her wails, and he made up his mind she was acting, because if she was not acting, and if the grief she felt was real, then it was excessive grief, and perhaps incurable. She was getting stronger every day, the doctor had said so, and she had better learn to control herself or she would be a nervous wreck. And it wasn't a bit like her, to have no thought for him, or for what he might be suffering. It wasn't like her at all. She was always kind. He began to fear she would never be the same. He would have liked to kneel down beside the bed and talk to her in a very quiet voice, and make her understand that he knew what she was going through, and that he was going through much the same thing himself, and to ask her not to shut him away from her. But he felt afraid of her, and in any case Mrs. Knox was in the room. He was helpless. He was trying to think of something to say, not to walk out in silence, when Mrs. Knox came around the end of the bed and touched his arm familiarly, as though they were conspirators.

"The poor child is upset," she said. "We'll leave her by herself awhile, and then I'll bring her up something to eat. Now, you go along down. I have your own tea all ready."

Delia turned her head on the pillow and looked at him. "Martin," she said, "I am not angry with you."

He would have gone to her then, but Mrs. Knox spoke at once. "We know you're not angry, Mrs. Bagot," she said. "Now, you rest yourself, and I'll be back in a minute with your tray." She gave Martin a little push to start him out of the room, and since Delia was already turning her face away, he walked out and down the stairs.

There seemed to be no end to the damage—even the house looked bleak and the furniture looked poor and cheap. It was only a year since they moved into the house, and it had all seemed lovely then. Only a year. He was beginning to fear that Delia had turned against him. He had visions of awful scenes and strains in the future, a miserable life. He wished they could go back to the beginning and start all over again, but the place where they had stood together, where they had been happy, was all trampled over and so spoiled that it seemed impossible ever to make it smooth again. And how could they even begin to make it smooth with this one memory, which they should have shared, standing like an enemy between them and making enemies out of them. He would not let himself think of the baby. He might never be able to forget the shape of the poor little defeated bundle he had carried out of the bedroom in his arms, and that he had cried over down here in the hall, but he was not going to let his mind dwell on it, not for one minute. He wanted Delia as she used to be. He wanted the girl who would never have struck out at him, or spoken roughly to him. He was beginning to see there were things about her that he had never guessed at and that he did not want to know about. He thought, Better

let her rest, and let this fit work itself out. Maybe tomorrow she'll
be herself again. He had a fancy that when he next approached
Delia it would be on tiptoe, going very quietly, hardly breathing,
moving into her presence without a sound that might startle her,
or surprise her, or even wake her up, so that he might find her
again as she had been the first time he saw her, quiet, untroubled,
hardly speaking, alone, altogether alone and all his.

Mrs. Bagot was telling the truth when she told Martin she
was not angry with him. It irritated her that he thought all he had
to do was put his arms around her and all her sorrow would go
away, but she wasn't really angry with him. What it was—he
held her so tightly that she was afraid she might lose sight of
the baby, and the fear made her frantic. The baby must not drift
out of sight, that was her only thought, and that is why she struck
out at Martin and begged to be left alone. As he walked out of
the room, she turned her face away so that he would not see
the tears beginning to pour down her face again. Then she slept.
When Martin came up to the room next time, she was asleep,
and not, as he suspected, pretending to be asleep, but he was
grateful for the pretense, if that is what it was, and he crept
away, back downstairs to his book.

Mrs. Bagot slept for a long time. When she woke up, the
room was dark and the house was silent. Outside was silent too;
she could hear nothing. This was the front bedroom, where she
and Martin slept together, and she lay in their big bed. The room
was made irregular by its windows—a bow window, and then,
in the flat section of wall that faced the door, French windows.
The French windows were partly open, and the long white net
curtains that covered them moved gently in a breeze Mrs. Bagot
could not feel. She had washed all the curtains last week, and
starched them, getting the room ready for the baby. In the dim
light of the street lamp, she could see the dark roof line of the
row of houses across the street, and beyond the houses a very
soft blackness, the sky. She was much calmer than she had been,
and she no longer feared that she would lose sight of the small

shape that had drifted, she noticed, much further away while she
slept. He was travelling a long way, but she would watch him.
She was his mother, and it was all she could do for him now. She
could do it. She was weak, and the world was very shaky, but
the light of other days shone steadily and showed the truth. She
was no longer bewildered, and the next time Martin came to
stand hopefully beside her bed she smiled at him and spoke to
him in her ordinary voice.

Anna Akhmatova
1889–1966

from *Requiem 1935–1940*

CRUCIFIXION

"Weep not for Me, Mother,
in the grave I have life."

I

The choir of angels glorified the great hour,
the heavens melted in flames.
He said to His Father: "Why hast Thou forsaken me?"
and to His Mother: "Oh, weep not for Me . . ."

II

Mary Magdalene smote her breast and wept,
the disciple whom He loved turned to stone,
but where the Mother stood in silence
nobody even dared look.

Translated from the Russian by Richard McKane

Charles Lamb
1775–1834

On an Infant Dying as Soon as Born

I saw where in the shroud did lurk
A curious frame of Nature's work.
A flow'ret crushed in the bud,
A nameless piece of Babyhood,
Was in her cradle-coffin lying;
Extinct, with scarce the sense of dying
So soon to exchange the imprisoning womb
For darker closets of the tomb!
She did but ope an eye, and put
A clear beam forth, then straight up shut
For the long dark: ne'er more to see
Through glasses of mortality.
Riddle of destiny, who can show
What thy short visit meant, or know
What thy errand here below?
Shall we say, that Nature blind
Check'd her hand, and changed her mind,
Just when she had exactly wrought
A finish'd pattern without fault?
Could she flag, or could she tire,
Or lack'd she the Promethean fire
(With her nine moons' long workings sicken'd)
That should thy little limbs have quicken'd?
Limbs so firm, they seem'd to assure
Life of health and days mature:
Woman's self in miniature!
Limbs so fair, they might supply
(Themselves now but cold imagery)
The sculptor to make Beauty by.
Or did the stern-eyed Fate descry,
That babe, or mother, one must die;

So in mercy left the stock,
And cut the branch; to save the shock
Of young years widow'd; and the pain
When Single State comes back again
To the lone man, who, 'reft of wife,
Thenceforward drags a maimed life?
The economy of Heaven is dark;
And wisest clerks have miss'd the mark,
Why Human Buds, like this, should fall,
More brief than fly ephemeral,
That has his day; while shrivell'd crones
Stiffen with age to stocks and stones;
And crabbed use the conscience sears
In sinners of an hundred years.
Mother's prattle, mother's kiss,
Baby fond, thou ne'er wilt miss.
Rites, which custom does impose,
Silver bells and baby clothes;
Coral redder than those lips,
Which pale death did late eclipse;
Music framed for infants' glee,
Whistle never tuned for thee;
Though thou want'st not, thou shalt have them,
Loving hearts were they which gave them.
Let not one be missing; nurse
See them laid upon the hearse
Of infant slain by doom perverse.
Why should kings and nobles have
Pictured trophies to their grave,
And we, churls, to thee deny
Thy pretty toys with thee to lie,
A more harmless vanity!

John Crowe Ransom
1888–1974

Bells for John Whiteside's Daughter

There was such speed in her little body,
And such lightness in her footfall,
It is no wonder her brown study
Astonishes us all.

Her wars were bruited in our high window.
We looked among orchard trees and beyond
Where she took arms against her shadow,
Or harried unto the pond

The lazy geese, like a snow cloud
Dripping their snow on the green grass,
Tricking and stopping, sleepy and proud,
Who cried in goose, Alas,

For the tireless heart within the little
Lady with rod that made them rise
From their noon apple-dreams and scuttle
Goose-fashion under the skies!

But now go the bells, and we are ready,
In one house we are sternly stopped
To say we are vexed at her brown study,
Lying so primly propped.

Theodore Roethke
1908–1963

Elegy for Jane

MY STUDENT, THROWN BY A HORSE

I remember the neckcurls, limp and damp as tendrils;
And her quick look, a sidelong pickerel smile;
And how, once startled into talk, the light syllables leaped
    for her,
And she balanced in the delight of her thought,
A wren, happy, tail into the wind,
Her song trembling the twigs and small branches.
The shade sang with her;
The leaves, their whispers turned to kissing;
And the mold sang in the bleached valleys under the rose.

Oh, when she was sad, she cast herself down into such a
    pure depth,
Even a father could not find her:
Scraping her cheek against straw;
Stirring the clearest water.

My sparrow, you are not here,
Waiting like a fern, making a spiny shadow.
The sides of wet stones cannot console me,
Nor the moss, wound with the last light.

If only I could nudge you from this sleep,
My maimed darling, my skittery pigeon.
Over this damp grave I speak the words of my love:
I, with no rights in this matter,
Neither father nor lover.

The Grief
of Children

Little is known about the way children comprehend death. The next selections address feelings the writers were unable to express in childhood, but that remain vivid in the memory of the adult. In speaking to a young child, Gerard Manley Hopkins reminds all mourners of an essential aspect of grief.

James Agee
1909–1955

This selection from *A Death in the Family* follows a scene in which the boy Rufus (Agee's childhood name) has disobeyed his aunt's orders to stay in the house, and goes out in the street to boast to some neighborhood bullies about his father's death as a way of gaining importance with them. Later, as the reality of the death begins to surface, Rufus castigates himself. With great understanding Agee reveals how guilt is incorporated into a child's sensibility when a parent dies.

So I tell them he is dead and they look up to me, they don't tease me.

Showing off because he's dead, that's all you can show off about. Any other thing they'd tease me and I wouldn't fight back.

How would your daddy like it?

But he likes me to get along with them. That's why I— went out—showed off.

He felt so uneasy, deep inside his stomach, that he could

not think about it any more. He wished he hadn't done it. He wished he could go back and not do anything of the kind. He wished his father could know about it and tell him that yes he was bad but it was all right he didn't mean to be bad. He was glad his father didn't know because if his father knew he would think even worse of him than ever. But if his father's soul was around, always, watching over them, then he knew. And that was worst of anything because there was no way to hide from a soul, and no way to talk to it, either. He just knows, and it couldn't say anything to him, and he couldn't say anything to it. It couldn't whip him either, but it could sit and look at him and be ashamed of him.

"I didn't mean it," he said aloud. "I didn't mean to do bad."

I wanted to show you my cap, he added, silently.

He looked at his father's morsechair.

Not a mark on his body.

He still looked at the chair. With a sense of deep stealth and secrecy he finally went over and stood beside it. After a few moments, and after listening most intently, to be sure that nobody was near, he smelled of the chair, its deeply hollowed seat, the arms, the back. There was only a cold smell of tobacco and, high along the back, a faint smell of hair. He thought of the ash tray on its weighted strap on the arm; it was empty. He ran his finger inside it; there was only a dim smudge of ash. There was nothing like enough to keep in his pocket or wrap up in a paper. He looked at his finger for a moment and licked it; his tongue tasted of darkness.

Edward Lucie-Smith

The Lesson

"Your father's gone," my bald headmaster said.
His shiny dome and brown tobacco jar
Splintered at once in tears. It wasn't grief.

I cried for knowledge which was bitterer
Than any grief. For there and then I knew
That grief has uses—that a father dead
Could bind the bully's fist a week or two;
And then I cried for shame, then for relief.

I was a month past ten when I learnt this:
I still remember how the noise was stilled
In school-assembly when my grief came in.
Some goldfish in a bowl quietly sculled
Around their shining prison on its shelf.
They were indifferent. All the other eyes
Were turned towards me. Somewhere in myself
Pride, like a goldfish, flashed a sudden fin.

Donald Justice

First Death

JUNE 12, 1933

I saw my grandmother grow weak.
When she died, I kissed her cheek.

I remember the new taste—
Powder mixed with a drying paste.

Down the hallway, on its table,
Lay the family's great Bible.

In the dark, by lamplight stirred,
The Void grew pregnant with the Word.

In black ink they wrote it down.
The older ink was turning brown.

From the woods there came a cry—
The hoot owl asking who, not why.

The men sat silent on the porch,
Each lighted pipe a friendly torch

Against the unknown and the known.
But the child knew himself alone.

JUNE 13, 1933
The morning sun rose up and stuck.
Sunflower strove with hollyhock.

I ran the worn path past the sty.
Nothing was hidden from God's eye.

The barn door creaked. I walked among
Chaff and wrinkled cakes of dung.

In the dim light I read the dates
On the dusty license plates

Nailed to the wall as souvenirs.
I breathed the dust in of the years.

I circled the abandoned Ford
Before I tried the running board.

At the wheel I felt the heat
Press upwards through the springless seat.

And when I touched the silent horn,
Small mice scattered through the corn.

JUNE 14, 1933
I remember the soprano
Fanning herself at the piano,

And the preacher looming large
Above me in his dark blue serge.

My shoes brought in a smell of clay
To mingle with the faint sachet

Of flowers sweating in their vases.
A stranger showed us to our places.

The stiff fan stirred in mother's hand.
Air moved, but only when she fanned.

I wondered how could all her grief
Be squeezed into one small handkerchief.

There was a buzzing on the sill.
It stopped, and everything was still.

We bowed our heads, we closed our eyes
To the mercy of the flies.

Vicente Aleixandre

My Grandfather's Death

I went by on tiptoe
and could still hear the painful breathing of the sick man.

And I sat down in my little-boy's room,
and I went to bed.
I could hear people entering and leaving the house, and way in
        the background,
like a murmur, the long sound of the tossing sea.

I dreamed that he and I were out in a boat.
And what fish we caught! And how beautiful the smooth sea was.
And what a fresh breeze under the long sunlight.
He had the same kind face as always,
and with his hand he pointed out the sparkles,
the hazy happy coastline, the little crests of water.
And how happy I was alone with him in the boat . . .
Alone with him, so big and so secure for me out there, alone
        with him on the sea.
"Let's not get there so soon!" . . . , I said. And he laughed.
He had white hair, as always, and those blue eyes they tell me I
        have too.
And he started to tell me a story. And I started to fall asleep.
Ah, rocked out there on the sea. With his voice pushing us
        along.
I slept and I dreamed his voice. A dream within a dream . . .
And I dreamed I was dreaming. And way inside, another dream.
        And deeper another, and another,
and I at the bottom dreaming him, with him beside me, and both
        of us flying further into the dream.

And suddenly the boat . . . As if it struck something.
I opened my eyes! (And no one, just my room.)
And there was an utter silence as of arrival.

                    Translated from the Spanish by Stephen Kessler

Tove Ditlevsen
1918–1976

Ditlevsen's parents' death when she was young cut a trench in her
life between security and the hardships to come. From a working-
class background, she left school at fourteen to support herself,

experienced three unsuccessful marriages and drug addiction, but still managed to produce thirty-two books of poetry, fiction, memoirs, children's stories and essays. She committed suicide in 1976.

Self Portrait 2

When you have
once had
a great joy
it lasts always
quivers gently
on the edge of all the
insecure adult days
subdues inherited dread
makes sleep deeper.

The bedroom was
an island of light
my father and mother
were painted
on the morning's wall.
They handed a shining
picture book toward me
they smiled to see
my immense joy.

I saw they were young
and happy for
each other
saw it for the first
saw it for the last time.
The world became eternally
divided into a before
and after.

I was five years old
since then everything
has changed.

Translated from the Danish by Ann Freeman

William Maxwell

In his partly autobiographical novel *So Long, See You Tomorrow*, Maxwell recounts the impact of his mother's death on father and son and their difficulties in expressing their feelings. The picture of the two walking the floor together is a haunting image of their restlessness after "the shine went out of everything."

The Period of Mourning

When my father was getting along in years and the past began to figure more in his conversation, I asked him one day what my mother was like. I knew what she was like as my mother but I thought it was time somebody told me what she was like as a person. To my surprise he said, "That's water over the dam," shutting me up but also leaving me in doubt, because of his abrupt tone of voice, whether he didn't after all this time have any feeling about her much, or did have but didn't think he ought to. In any case he didn't feel like talking about her to me.

Very few families escape disasters of one kind or another, but in the years between 1909 and 1919 my mother's family had more than its share of them. My grandfather, spending the night in a farmhouse, was bitten on the ear by a rat or a ferret and died three months later of blood poisoning. My mother's only brother was in an automobile accident and lost his right arm. My mother's younger sister poured kerosene on a grate fire that wouldn't burn and set fire to her clothing and bore the scars of this all the rest of her life. My older brother, when he was five years old, got his foot caught in a turning carriage wheel.

I was so small when these things happened that either I did not know about them or else I didn't feel them because they took place at one remove, so to speak. When my brother undressed at night he left his artificial leg leaning against a chair. It was as familiar to me, since we slept in the same room, as his cap or his baseball glove. He was not given to feeling sorry for himself, and older people were always careful not to show their sorrow over what had happened to him. What I felt about his "affliction" was tucked away in my unconscious mind (assuming there is such a thing) where I couldn't get at it.

My younger brother was born on New Year's Day, at the height of the influenza epidemic of 1918. My mother died two days later of double pneumonia. After that, there were no more disasters. The worst that could happen had happened, and the shine went out of everything. Disbelieving, we endured the wreath on the door, and the undertaker coming and going, the influx of food, the overpowering odor of white flowers, and all the rest of it, including the first of a series of housekeepers, who took care of the baby and sat in my mother's place at mealtime. Looking back I think it more than likely that long before she ever laid eyes on us that sallow-faced, flat-chested woman had got the short end of the stick. She came from a world we knew nothing about, and I don't remember that she ever had any days off. She may have made a stab at being a mother to my older brother and me, but it would have taken a good deal more than that to break through our resistance. We knew what we had had, and were not going to be taken in by any form of counterfeit affection.

My mother's sisters and my father's sisters and my grandmother all watched over us. If they hadn't, I don't know what would have become of us, in that sad house, where nothing ever changed, where life had come to a standstill. My father was all but undone by my mother's death. In the evening after supper he walked the floor and I walked with him, with my arm around his waist. I was ten years old. He would walk from the living room into the front hall, then, turning, past the grandfather's clock and on into the library, and from the library into the living room. Or he would walk from the library into the dining room and then into the living room by another doorway, and back to the front hall. Because he didn't say anything, I didn't either. I only tried to sense, as he was about to turn, which room he was going to next so we wouldn't bump into each other. His eyes were focused on things not in those rooms, and his face was the color of ashes. From conversations that had taken place in front of me I knew he was tormented by the belief that he was responsible for what had happened. If he had only taken this or that precaution . . . It wasn't true, any of it. At a time when the epidemic was raging and people were told to avoid crowds, he and my mother got on a crowded train in order to go to Bloomington, thirty miles away, where the hospital facilities were better than in Lincoln. But even if she had had the baby at home, she still would have caught the flu. My older brother or my father or I would have given it to her. We all came down with it.

I had to guess what my older brother was thinking. It was not something he cared to share with me. I studied the look in his hazel eyes and was startled: If I hadn't known, I would have thought that he'd had his feelings hurt by something he was too proud to talk about. It was the most he could manage in the way of concealment. At night we undressed and got into bed and fell asleep without taking advantage of the dark to unburden our hearts to each other. It strikes me as strange now. It didn't then. Though we were very different, he knew me inside out—that is to say, he knew my weaknesses and how to play on them, and this had made me leery about exposing my feelings to him. I also suspect that I had told on him once too often. I have no way of knowing what he might have said. What I didn't say, across the few feet that separated our two beds, was that I couldn't understand how it had happened to us. It seemed like a mistake. And mistakes ought to be rectified, only this one couldn't be.

Between the way things used to be and the way they were now was a void that couldn't be crossed. I had to find an explanation other than the real one, which was that we were no more immune to misfortune than anybody else, and the idea that kept recurring to me, perhaps because of that pacing the floor with my father, was that I had inadvertently walked through a door that I shouldn't have gone through and couldn't get back to the place I hadn't meant to leave. Actually, it was the other way round: I hadn't gone anywhere and nothing was changed, so far as the roof over our heads was concerned, it was just that she was in the cemetery.

When I got home from school I did what I had always done, which was to read, curled up in the window seat in the library or lying flat on my back on the floor with my feet in a chair, in the darkest corner I could find. The house was full of places to read that fitted me like a glove, and I read the same books over and over. Children tend to derive comfort and support from the totally familiar—an umbrella stand, a glass ashtray backed with brightly colored cigar bands, the fire tongs, anything. With the help of these and other commonplace objects—with the help also of the two big elm trees that shaded the house from the heat of the sun, and the trumpet vine by the back door, and the white lilac bush by the dining-room window, and the comfortable wicker porch furniture and the porch swing that contributed its *creak . . . creak . . .* to the sounds of the summer night—I got from one day to the next.

My father got from one day to the next by attending faithfully to his job. He was the state agent for a small fire insurance company and traveled from one end of Illinois to the other, inspecting risks and cultivating the friendship of local agents so they would give more business to his company. On Saturday morning, sitting in the library, he would put a check on each inspection slip as he finished glancing over it, and when he had a pile of them he would hand them to me and I would sit on the floor and arrange them around me alphabetically, by towns, proud that I could be of use to him. He left on Tuesday morning, carrying a grip that was heavy with printed forms, and came home Friday afternoon to a household that was seething with problems he was not accustomed to dealing with. His sadness was of the kind that is patient and without hope. He continued to sleep in the bed he and my mother had shared, and tried to act in a way she would have wanted him to, and I suspect that as time passed he was less and less sure what that was. He gave away her jewelry, and more important to me, her clothes, so I could no longer open her closet door and look at them.

I overheard one family friend after another assuring him that there was no cure but time, and though he said, "Yes, I know," I could tell he didn't believe them. Once a week he would wind all the clocks in the house, beginning with the grandfather's clock in the front hall. Their minute and hour hands went round dependably and the light outside corroborated what they said: it was breakfast time, it was late afternoon, it was night, with the darkness pressing against the windowpanes. What the family friends said is true. For some people. For others the hands of the clock can go round till kingdom come and not cure anything. I don't know by what means my father came to terms with his grief. All I know is that it was more than a year before the color came back into his face and he could smile when somebody said something funny.

When people spoke about my mother it was always in generalities—her wonderful qualities, her gift for making those around her happy, and so on—that didn't tell me anything I didn't know before. It was as if they couldn't see her clearly for what had happened to her. And to us. She didn't like having her picture taken and all we had was a few snapshots and one formal photograph, taken when she was in her early twenties, with her hair piled on top of her head and a black velvet ribbon around her throat. She was only thirty-eight when she died, but she had grown heavy, as women of that period tended to do. There was no question about the mouth or the soft brown eyes. The rest I did not recognize, though I was willing to believe that she had once looked like that. This picture didn't satisfy my father either, and he got the photographer who had taken it to touch it up so she would look more like a mature woman. The result was something I was quite sure my mother had never looked like—vague and idealized and as if she might not even remember who we were. My mother sometimes got excited and flew off the handle, but not this woman, who died before her time, leaving a grief-stricken husband and three motherless children. The retouched photograph came between me and the face I remembered, and it got harder and harder to recall my mother as she really was. After I couldn't remember any more except in a general way what she looked like, I could still remember the sound of her voice, and I clung to that. I also clung to the idea that if things remained exactly the way they were, if we were careful not to take a step in any direction from the place where we were now, we would somehow get back to the way it was before she died. I knew that this was not a rational belief, but the alternative—that when people die they are really gone and I would never see her again—was more than I could manage then or for a long time afterward.

When my father was an old man, he surprised me by remarking that he understood what my mother's death meant to me but had no idea what to do about it. I think it would have been something if he had just said this. If he didn't, it was possibly because he thought there was nothing he or anybody else could do. Or he may have thought I would reject any help he tried to give me.

Stanley Kunitz
1905–1980

The Portrait

My mother never forgave my father
for killing himself,

especially at such an awkward time
and in a public park,
that spring
when I was waiting to be born.
She locked his name
in her deepest cabinet
and would not let him out,
though I could hear him thumping.
When I came down from the attic
with the pastel portrait in my hand
of a long-lipped stranger
with a brave moustache
and deep brown level eyes,
she ripped it into shreds
without a single word
and slapped me hard.
In my sixty-fourth year
I can feel my cheek
still burning.

Herbert Mason

from *Gilgamesh*

I asked unanswerable questions a child asks
When a parent dies—for nothing. Only slowly
Did I make myself believe—or hope—they
Might all be swept up in their fragments
Together
And made whole again
By some compassionate hand.
But my hand was too small
To do the gathering.
I have only known this feeling since

When I looked out across the sea of death,
This pull inside against a littleness—myself
Waiting for an upward gesture.

Gerard Manley Hopkins
1844–1889

Spring and Fall: To a Young Child

Márgarét, are you gríeving
Over Goldengrove unleaving?
Leáves, like the things of man, you
With your fresh thought care for, can you?
Áh, ás the heart grows older
It will come to such sights colder
By and by, nor spare a sigh
Though worlds of wanwood leafmeal lie;
And yet you will weep and know why.
Now no matter, child, the name:
Sórrow's spríngs áre the same.
Nor mouth had, no nor mind, expressed
What heart heard of, ghost guessed:
It ís the blight man was born for,
It is Margaret you mourn for.

Spring

Each substance of a grief hath twenty shadows.
  —William Shakespeare, *Richard II*

Ah woe is me! Winter is come and gone,
But grief returns with the revolving year.
  —Percy Bysshe Shelley, *Adonais*

What restraint or limit should there be to grief
for one so dear?
                         —Horace, *Ode XXIV*

Those who grieve find comfort in weeping and
in arousing their sorrow until the body is too
tired to bear the inner emotions.
           —Maimonides, *Regimen Moreh Nebukim*
             (*Guide of the Perplexed*)

Grief tires more than anything, and brings a
deeper slumber.
       —George Louis Palmella Busson Du Maurier,
       Trilby, Part VIII

The Middle Period of Mourning

When the anger and bewilderment of first grief subside, the true labor of mourning begins. This period of depression may set in after a few weeks or months, or even years later, if grief has been repressed.

This is the phase of searching for the dead person. The writers in this section describe the necessary restlessness and disarray of this season of depression and the gradual movement toward reassembling what was valuable in the past as they move forward into the future.

William Carlos Williams
1883–1963

The Widow's Lament in Springtime

Sorrow is my own yard
where the new grass
flames as it has flamed
often before but not
with the cold fire
that closes round me this year.
Thirtyfive years
I lived with my husband.
The plumtree is white today
with masses of flowers.
Masses of flowers

loaded the cherry branches
and color some bushes
yellow and some red
but the grief in my heart
is stronger than they
for though they were my joy
formerly, today I notice them
and turned away forgetting.
Today my son told me
that in the meadows,
at the edge of the heavy woods
in the distance, he saw
trees of white flowers.
I feel that I would like
to go there
and fall into those flowers
and sink into the marsh near them.

Robert Bridges
1844–1930

Elegy

The wood is bare; a river-mist is steeping
    The trees that winter's chill of life bereaves;
Only their stiffened boughs break silence, weeping
    Over their fallen leaves;

That lie upon the dank earth brown and rotten,
    Miry and matted in the soaking wet—
Forgotten with spring, that is forgotten
    By them that can forget.

Yet it was here we walked when ferns were springing,
  And through the mossy bank shot bud and blade—
Here found in summer, when the birds were singing,
  A green and pleasant shade.

'T'was here we loved in sunnier days and greener;
  And now, in this disconsolate decay,
I come to see her where I most have seen her,
  And touch the happier day.

For on this path, at every turn and corner,
  The fancy of her figure on me falls;
Yet walks she with the slow step of a mourner,
  Nor hears my voice that calls.

So through my heart there winds a track of feeling,
  A path of memory, that is all her own,
Whereto her phantom beauty ever stealing
  Haunts the sad spot alone.

About her steps the trunks are bare; the branches
  Drip heavy tears upon her downcast head,
And bleed from unseen wounds that no sun stanches,
  For the year's sun is dead.

And dead leaves wrap the fruits that summer planted;
  And birds that love the South have taken wing.
The wanderer, loitering o'er the scene enchanted,
  Weeps, and despairs of spring.

Robert Browning
1812–1889

This poem is in memory of Browning's cousin and boyhood companion, who died in May, 1852. The plant that appears in Dul-
wich Wood at that time of year is the spotted persicaria, which
legend says grew beneath the Cross and received its purple spots
from the blood of Christ.

May and Death

I wish that when you died last May,
   Charles, there had died along with you
Three parts of spring's delightful things;
   Aye, and, for me, the fourth part too.

A foolish thought, and worse, perhaps!
   There must be many a pair of friends
Who, arm in arm, deserve the warm
   Moon-births and the long evening-ends.

So, for their sake, be May still May!
   Let their new time, as mine of old,
Do all it did for me; I bid
   Sweet sights and sounds throng manifold.

Only, one little sight, one plant,
   Woods have in May, that starts up green
Save a sole streak which, so to speak,
   Is spring's blood, spilt its leaves between—

That, they might spare; a certain wood
   Might miss the plant; their loss were small;
But I—whene'er the leaf grows there,
   Its drop comes from my heart, that's all.

Dante Gabriel Rossetti
1828–1882

from *The House of Life*

83. BARREN SPRING

Once more the changed year's turning wheel returns:
   And as a girl sails balanced in the wind,
   And now before and now again behind
Stoops as it swoops, with cheek that laughs and burns—
So Spring comes merry towards me here, but earns
   No answering smile from me, whose life is twined
   With the dead boughs that winter still must bind,
And whom to-day the Spring no more concerns.

Behold, this crocus is a withering flame;
   This snowdrop, snow; this apple-blossom's part
   To breed the fruit that breeds the serpent's art.
Nay, for these Spring-flowers, turn thy face from them,
Nor gaze till on the year's last lily-stem
   The white cup shrivels round the golden heart.

Toby Talbot

from *A Book About My Mother*

Grief comes in unexpected surges. As when nursing, and anything can trigger the onrush of milk. An infant in a carriage or a child crying, but also a traffic light changing, water running, a dog barking. . . . Little alarms these are, transmitted to that network of nerves, muscle, hormone, tissue, and cells that constitute the physical self. Mysterious cues that set off a reminder of grief. It comes crashing like a wave, sweeping me in its crest, twisting me inside out. Then recedes, leaving me broken. Oh, Mama, I don't want to eat, to walk, to get out of bed. Reading, working,

cooking, listening, mothering. Nothing matters. I do not want
to be distracted from my grief. I wouldn't mind dying. I wouldn't
mind it at all. I wake from sleep in the middle of every night and
say to myself, "My mother is dead!" ...

Mourning in many ways is like falling in love. An isola-
tion, an impoverishment, a shrinking, a contraction of concerns
and interests. . . . It represses all other feelings and life contents.
You seem to be filled with it. Always. In a sense, like pregnancy.
But unlike the quickening of pregnancy, here a lead weight lodges
in your stomach. Whereas pregnancy imparts a sense of doing
something even while inactive, mourning bequeaths a sense of
futility and meaninglessness in the midst of activity. It creates
disorder in your network of mental habits. I write on the black-
board, read a book, screen a film, pare carrots, speak on the
telephone. Phantom gestures, flickers on an empty screen. Her
death is the only thing on my mind. . . .

How to soften the pain of upheaval. Making love, the
supreme remedy for anguish: To make love is to plunge into
the world prior to birth, prior to the greatest separation. To unite
and reunite, to generate birth and be reborn. It is to find again
that deep slowness, that wordless rhythm, that tidal dissolve.
Darkness. Silence. Time suspended. Flesh unto flesh. Breath unto
breath. My ear upon my husband's heart ausculates the steady
beat of life . . . He curls around me. I become part of his smell.
Two bodies entwined, throbbing, melting into a primal cocoon.
Making love is the great regression. The great reunion. Blood,
sweat, sperm. Birth, copulation, death. A race, a shared frenzy.
Air rushing into the lungs. Quivering fire. A spasm of existence. . . .

[Five months after her mother's death]

I must not, I tell myself, hurt my family. Impose my suffering. Depression is contagious. With a bad headache, any bad
hurt, it's best to go into your room and shut the door till the

hurt goes away. Excessive mourning is nonproductive, someone remarks. A social inconvenience, downright inconsiderate in the public eye. Life, according to my Orientalist friend, is a passage, a corridor, and she bids me to rid myself of morbid brooding.

Bullshit! I'm angry. It's all a rotten hoax, this life of ours. You go from zero to zero. Why attach yourself to love only to have your beloved ripped from you? The upshot of love is pain. Life is a death sentence. Better not to give yourself to anything. The more you give, the more is taken from you. It's like stitching away only to discover at the end of the seam that you had no knot at the other end of the thread. . . .

At times I think to myself: She wouldn't have wanted to bequeath a legacy of disintegration. I can see her tossing me one of her shrewd looks and saying, "Come on, snap out of it!"

Even now, as I think of her, that familiar swelling constricts my throat, turns it into a lump of clay, which means I can cry. But in the throes of tears, memories inevitably get foreshortened. Reduced to freeze shots of her in the hospital, in the coffin. Then again, silently, incredulously, I have to begin from the beginning and repeat: She's dead. As if it's just struck me. And I find myself drowning, engulfed by the disorder of the current, wanting to seize her hand to bring me to shore. Missing her so. Futilely trying to recapture that profile of elusive contours and shapes. To crystallize that deceased being. To evoke that palpable presence, the voice, inflections, and rhythms, the silences, expressions, gestures, stance, gait, the birthmarks and quirks. But the subject, prey like a shadow figure to shifting forms and arbitrary juxtapositions, omissions and simplifications, becomes indistinct.

And then the idealization. Another distortion. Idealizing her in a way antithetical to her nature. Bella was no lofty madonna, no enigmatic Mary, no *mater dolorosa.* She was a flesh-and-blood lady who got her hands wet, whose life encompassed pain and suffering. A human being with human flaws. It's a betrayal to remember only the good parts. . . .

* * *

A distinguishing characteristic of the human mammal: the prolonged dependency of the offspring on maternal protection. All mothers are not motherly. Some motherly mothers are over-protective. Trespassers on their children's lives. Refusing to let go.

Bella was motherly, but not overprotective. . . .

My mother's world was different from mine. That was clear. To her and to me. Her world, I dreamed of transcending. It was her wish as well. She knew her limitations, understood the source of those limitations, knew that certain deprivations were irrevocable, but held no one to blame. Bella understood herself in her own existence. . . .

Bella in many ways was the ideal traditional mother. All-giving, all-forgiving, all-caring, all-dedicated. The children came first.

Mothers serve as models for their daughters. A grown daughter thinks, What would she have wanted? What would she have done? When she is acting contrary to her mother's presumed desire, the daughter's anxiety is aroused. Loss of mother's approval still matters.

Unwittingly, Bella may have pressed me too far in my own motherliness. I was trying to emulate that old pattern. To be the perfect mother. At the same time, I did not want to lose the thread of the individual I was before motherhood. Not to betray my true self. Result: conflict and guilt often nagged intrusively at my work.

It was a juggling act. To nurse and, in between nursings, hurry off to a class. To lay a child in for her nap, then sneak off to a quiet corner to translate, write, or read, ear always cocked for some untoward infantile squeak. . . . In my mind, I was always in two places at once. "You can't be at two weddings with one backside," she used to say. But I always was. . . .

Bella identified herself primarily as a mother. This realization prompts me to reflect: Did I adequately repay her? Is my grief in part a sense of something owed her? What will I expect of my daughters when I am old?

[The summer after Bella's death in February]

Mourning has a path of its own. A route which does not move in one straight line. Some days I can look at her photograph and the image revives her, reinforces her for me. On other days I gaze at her and am blinded with tears. Newly bereft.

What is it that I mourn? Her loss of life? The end of her pleasures? The fact that never again will she drink a glass of sweet country water, or bask in the sun, or set eyes upon her grandchildren, never again steep in a hot bath, or sip a cup of too hot coffee?

Or is it my own loss that I mourn? My insatiability for her physical presence? The knowledge that she's in the next room, in the next house, in the next city. As when I was a child bedridden with a cold, knowing she was within reach of my voice, that I could bask in her calm, her vigilance and cheer. . . .

Or perhaps I mourn the loss of my childhood and youth, of my past . . . I mourn her record of me. Her support, her corroboration, her assurance that when things were bad, they'd get better.

Am I clinging to some youthful version of myself? Or is it my loss of innocence that I mourn? The knowledge that I have changed.

These notes are an umbilical cord. A way of being with her still. Of bringing her close. A release of a deep well of sorrow. Not a work of imagination, with plot or argument, but one of pain . . . Their order, like mourning, like memory, does not move in a straight course, in a continous day-by-day sequence.

Once my daughter Nina at the age of four was weeping bitterly. In trying to comfort her, I brushed the tears from her cheeks. Her sobs immediately converted into an angered outcry: "Give me back my tears!"

Mourning has its ways. As Ovid said, "Truly, it is allowed to weep. By weeping, we disperse our wrath; and tears go through the heart, even like a stream."

I meet casual acquaintances, people I haven't seen for some time. They ask the simple question: How are you? And instead of replying with a wry, Don't ask, as she might have, my news comes tumbling forth. Like a murderer who has a need to tell about his crime. How is it possible to talk of anything else? Do you know? Have you heard? Can you tell? *It alone is true.* Why am I telling it? For sympathy? To be pitied as a small child? Only she could pity me as I wish to be pitied. *Mama sheinenkeh*, she might say, and that in itself would comfort me. Is it to let acquaintances know that I'm not the same person? Insinuating that they handle me with caution? Reassess me? What can anyone say? Or is it to assert my specialness, my special grief? Vanity, in short.

[Late summer]

Am I healing? I'm able to gaze at her photograph without that tourniquet tightening round my throat, clamping memory. Without hot tears flooding my eyes. Tears that blur the image, obliterate the past. When you try so hard to trace every feature, the profile inevitably gets lost. I find myself now able to look at that closeup of her and to discern the jolly glint, the animated stance, the practical gaze, the calm look. I can find comfort, not merely agony. I need to look at her picture less, and I see more. I'm beginning to see her in *her* life, and not only myself bereft of her life. I can hear her saying with a little smile: *Enough. Don't cry. Be a mensh! You have your life ahead of you.* Who was it that said: A mother is not to lean on, but to make leaning unnecessary?

[Fall]

She was the *mysterium tremendum* of life.

But that season is over.

Slowly I find myself being weaned from her material presence. Yet filled with her as never before. It is I now who represent us both. I am our mutual past. I am my mother and my self. She gave me love, to love myself, and to love the world. I must remember how to love.

Piece by piece, I reenter the world. A new phase. A new body, a new voice. Birds console me by flying, trees by growing, dogs by the warm patch they leave on the sofa. Unknown people merely by performing their motions. It's like a slow recovery from a sickness, this recovery of one's self. The old self, that bustling, jaunty, smiling, compliant version, turns the corner and vanishes. Gone is that pinch-penny effort to accordion each calendar day. Time is a gift rather than a goad. Diminished is concern about people's opinions, abandoned the notion of perfection, the illusion that children can be spared grief and disappointment. . . .

My life now is only mine.

She was the one who taught me to love and to receive love. To be unafraid. In her life and in the way she met death. My mother was at peace. She was ready. A free woman. "Let me go," she said. Okay, Mama, I'm letting you go.

Widows and Widowers

This is the one class of mourner given a specific title. "Widow" comes from the Latin *videre*, "to separate," and the Sanskrit *vindhate*, "he lacks." The loss of a lover and life companion alters a hundred details of daily existence and communication; it also obliges the widowed to commence the task of recovering an identity separate from the one to whom they have surrendered a part of themselves. In the next selections, the poems isolate specific feelings of sadness and loneliness; the journals and memoirs describe the process of the journey to a new self.

Li Ch'ing Chao
1084–1151

Li Ch'ing Chao is known as China's greatest female poet.

P'u-Shen Sheng Man

Unending search in endless quest
So cold and still, how cold and still;
By grief and anguish, grief and anguish hard oppressed.
This season of the sudden change from warm to chill
Weighs down the heart in search of peace.
Cupfuls of light wine, two or three;
How else confront the wind that blows at dusk so urgently?
Even the flighting geese
Have stabbed me to the heart,
Friends that fly past me out of older memories.

Chrysanthemums in yellow masses everywhere:
    Melancholy has marked them for its own.
For whom are they worth gathering growing there?
    Watching from my window all alone
How am I to live until the darkness falls?
Fine rain is falling, too, into the wu t'ung trees;
Plodding drop by drop down into the dusk's uncertainties.
    Tell me, with this, then, with all this,
How can the one word "sorrow" paint what sorrow is?

             Translated from the Chinese by Duncan Mackintosh;
                       rendered into verse by Alan Ayling

C. S. Lewis
1898–1963

Lewis originally published this private journal under the pseud-
onym N. W. Clerk, a pun on Old English for "I know not
what scholar."

from *A Grief Observed*

No one ever told me that grief felt so like fear. I am not afraid,
but the sensation is like being afraid. The same fluttering in the
stomach, the same restlessness, the yawning. I keep on swallowing.

At other times it feels like being mildly drunk, or concussed.
There is a sort of invisible blanket between the world and me. I
find it hard to take in what anyone says. Or perhaps, hard to
want to take it in. It is so uninteresting. Yet I want the others to
be about me. I dread the moments when the house is empty. If
only they would talk to one another and not to me.

There are moments, most unexpectedly, when something inside me tries to assure me that I don't really mind so much, not so very much, after all. Love is not the whole of a man's life. I was happy before I ever met H. I've plenty of what are called "resources." People get over these things. Come, I shan't do so badly. One is ashamed to listen to this voice but it seems for a little to be making out a good case. Then comes a sudden jab of red-hot memory and all this "commonsense" vanishes like an ant in the mouth of a furnace. . . .

And no one ever told me about the laziness of grief. Except at my job—where the machine seems to run much as usual—I loathe the slightest effort. Not only writing but even reading a letter is too much. Even shaving. What does it matter now whether my cheek is rough or smooth? They say an unhappy man wants distractions—something to take him out of himself. Only as a dog-tired man wants an extra blanket on a cold night; he'd rather lie there shivering than get up and find one. It's easy to see why the lonely become untidy; finally, dirty and disgusting. . . .

I cannot talk to the children about her. The moment I try, there appears on their faces neither grief, nor love, nor fear, nor pity, but the most fatal of all non-conductors, embarrassment. They look as if I were committing an indecency. They are longing for me to stop. I felt just the same after my own mother's death when my father mentioned her. I can't blame them. It's the way boys are. . . .

It isn't only the boys either. An odd by-product of my loss is that I'm aware of being an embarrassment to everyone I meet. At work, at the club, in the street, I see people, as they approach me, trying to make up their minds whether they'll "say something about it" or not. I hate it if they do, and if they don't. Some funk it altogether. R. has been avoiding me for a week. I like best the well brought-up young men, almost boys, who walk up to me as if I were a dentist, turn very red, get it over, and then edge away to the bar as quickly as they decently can.

Perhaps the bereaved ought to be isolated in special settlements like lepers. . . .

. . . There is one place where her absence comes locally home to me, and it is a place I can't avoid. I mean my own body. It had such a different importance while it was the body of H.'s lover. Now it's like an empty house. But don't let me deceive myself. This body would become important to me again, and pretty quickly, if I thought there was anything wrong with it. . . .

It is hard to have patience with people who say "There is no death" or "Death doesn't matter." There is death. And whatever is matters. And whatever happens has consequences, and it and they are irrevocable and irreversible. You might as well say that birth doesn't matter. I look up at the night sky. Is anything more certain that in all those vast times and spaces, if I were allowed to search them, I should nowhere find her face, her voice, her touch? She died. She is dead. Is the word so difficult to learn? . . .

Talk to me about the truth of religion and I'll listen gladly. Talk to me about the duty of religion and I'll listen submissively. But don't come talking to me about the consolations of religion or I shall suspect that you don't understand.

. . . Aren't all these notes the senseless writings of a man who won't accept the fact that there is nothing we can do with suffering except to suffer it? Who still thinks there is some device (if only he could find it) which will make pain not to be pain. It doesn't really matter whether you grip the arms of the dentist's chair or let your hands lie in your lap. The drill drills on. . . .

It's not true that I'm always thinking of H. Work and conversation make that impossible. But the times when I'm not are perhaps my worst. For then, though I have forgotten the reason, there is spread over everything a vague sense of wrongness, of something amiss. Like in those dreams where nothing terrible occurs—nothing that would sound even remarkable if you told it at breakfast-time—but the atmosphere, the taste of the whole thing is deadly. So with this. I see the rowan berries reddening and don't know for a moment why they, of all things, should be depressing. I hear a clock strike and some quality it always had before has gone out of the sound. What's wrong with the world to make it so flat, shabby, worn-out looking? Then I remember.

What sort of lover am I to think so much about my affliction and so much less about hers? Even the insane call, "Come back," is all for my own sake. I never even raised the question whether such a return, if it were possible, would be good for her. I want her back as an ingredient in the restoration of *my* past. Could I have wished her anything worse? Having got once through death, to come back and then, at some later date, have all her dying to do over again? They call Stephen the first martyr. Hadn't Lazarus the rawer deal? . . .

Something quite unexpected has happened. It came this morning early. For various reasons, not in themselves all mysterious, my heart was lighter than it had been for many weeks. For one thing, I suppose I am recovering physically from a good deal of mere exhaustion. And I'd had a very tiring but very healthy twelve hours the day before, and a sounder night's sleep; and after ten days of low-hung grey skies and motionless warm dampness, the sun was shining and there was a light breeze. And suddenly at the very moment when, so far, I mourned H. least, I remembered her best. Indeed it was something (almost) better than memory; an instantaneous, unanswerable impression. To say it was like a meeting would be going too far. Yet there was that in it which tempts one to use those words. It was as if the lifting of sorrow removed a barrier.

Why has no one told me these things? How easily I might have misjudged another man in the same situation? I might have said, "He's got over it. He's forgotten his wife," when the truth was, "He remembers her better *because* he has partly got over it."

. . . There's no denying that in some sense I "feel better," and with that comes at once a sort of shame, and a feeling that one is under a sort of obligation to cherish and foment and prolong one's unhappiness. I've read about that in books, but I never dreamed I should feel it myself. I am sure. H. wouldn't approve of it. She'd tell me not to be a fool. . . .

This is the fourth—and the last—empty MS. book I can find in the house; at least nearly empty, for there are some pages of very ancient arithmetic at the end by J. I resolve to let this limit my jottings. I *will not* start buying books for this purpose. In so far as this record was a defence against total collapse, a safety-valve, it has done some good. The other end I had in view turns out to have been based on a misunderstanding. I thought I could describe a *state*; make a map of sorrow. Sorrow, however, turns out to be not a state but a process. It needs not a map but a history, and if I don't stop writing that history at some quite arbitrary point, there's no reason why I should ever stop. There is something new to be chronicled every day. Grief is like a long valley, a winding valley where any bend may reveal a totally new landscape. As I've already noted, not every bend does. Sometimes the surprise is the opposite one; you are presented with exactly the same sort of country you thought you had left behind miles ago. That is when you wonder whether the valley isn't a circular trench. But it isn't. There are partial recurrences, but the sequence doesn't repeat.

Here, for instance, is a new phase, a new loss. I do all the walking I can, for I'd be a fool to go to bed not tired. Today I have been revisiting old haunts, taking in one of the long rambles that made me happy in my bachelor days. And this time the face of nature was not emptied of its beauty and the world didn't look (as I complained some days ago) like a mean street. On the contrary, every horizon, every stile or clump of trees, summoned me into a past kind of happiness, my pre-H. happiness. But the invitation seemed to me horrible. The happiness into which it invited me was insipid. I find that I don't want to go back again and be happy in *that* way. It frightens me to think that a mere going back should even be possible. For this fate would seem to me the worst of all; to reach a state in which my years of love and marriage should appear in retrospect a charming episode—like a holiday—that had briefly interrupted my interminable life and returned me to normal, unchanged. And then it would come to seem unreal—something so foreign to the usual texture of my history that I could almost believe it had happened to someone else. Thus H. would die to me a second time; a worse bereavement than the first. Anything but that. . . .

It is often thought that the dead see us. And we assume, whether reasonably or not, that if they see us at all they see us more clearly than before. Does H. now see exactly how much froth or tinsel there was in what she called, and I call, my love? So be it. Look your hardest, dear. I wouldn't hide it if I could. We didn't idealize each other. We tried to keep no secrets. You knew most of the rotten places in me already. If you now see anything worse, I can take it. So can you. Rebuke, explain, mock, forgive. For this is one of the miracles of love; it gives—to both, but perhaps especially to the woman—a power of seeing through its own enchantments and yet not being disenchanted. . . .

I said, several notebooks ago, that even if I got what seemed like an assurance of H.'s presence, I wouldn't believe it. Easier said than done. Even now, though, I won't treat anything of that sort as evidence. It's the *quality* of last night's experience—not what it proves but what it was—that makes it worth putting down. It was quite incredibly unemotional. Just the impression of her *mind* momentarily facing my own. Mind, not "soul" as we tend to think of soul. Certainly the reverse of what we call "soulful." Not at all like a rapturous re-union of lovers. Much more like getting a telephone call or a wire from her about some practical arrangement. Not that there was any "message"—just intelligence and attention. No sense of joy or sorrow. No love even, in our ordinary sense. No un-love. I had never in any mood imagined the dead as being so—well, so business-like. Yet there was an extreme and cheerful intimacy. An intimacy that had not passed through the senses or the emotions at all.

P'An Yueh (P'An Yeng Jen)
Fourth Century A.D.

In Mourning for His Dead Wife

Winter and Spring have come and gone.
Once more Autumn overtakes
Summer. She has returned to
The Hidden Springs. And all the
World separates us forever.
Who will listen to my secrets
Now? Who will I live for now?
I try to do my job at Court,
And reluctantly go through
The motions of duty, and
Take up the tasks I had dropped.
When I come home I can think
Only of her. When I come
In our room I expect to see her.
I catch her shadow on the
Screens and curtains. Her letters
Are the most precious examples
Of calligraphy. Her perfume
Still haunts the bedroom. Her clothes
Still hang there in the closet.
She is always alive in
My dreams. I wake with a start.

She vanishes. And I
Am overwhelmed with sorrow.
Two birds made a nest and then
There was only one. A pair
Of fishes were separated
And lost in the current.
The Autumn wind blows. The morning
Is misty, with dripping eaves.
All through the troubled night I was
Not able to forget in sleep.
I hope the time will come when
I am calm enough to beat
On a pot like Chuang Tsu did
In morning for his dead wife.

Translated from the Chinese by Kenneth Rexroth

Taniguchi Buson
1716–1783

Haiku

I feel a sudden chill—
In our bedroom, my dead wife's comb,
Underfoot.

Caitlin Thomas

The tumultuous sixteen-year marriage of Caitlin and Dylan
Thomas ended in 1953 with the death from acute alcoholism of
the celebrated Welsh poet while they were visiting the United

States. After a period of emotional paralysis, his widow accompanied his body back to Laugharne, the small village in Wales where he is buried and where for a time she continued to live. This selection from her 1957 memoir, *Leftover Life to Kill*, spills out the spiritual chaos she experienced on this funerary island where, friendless and utterly without support from a community, she seems to be acting out some ancient rite of mourners of befoulment of the flesh and tearing her hair.

---

from *Leftover Life to Kill*

Dylan and dying, Dylan and dying, they don't go together; or is it that they were bound to go together; he said so often enough, but I did not heed him. I was as foolish as women are supposed to be, the traditional woman, paid no attention, took him for granted, was only concerned with how to express my own aggressive, demanding, frustrated, vile, jealous self. And look what he has done to me! How brutally cruelly am I punished; surely out of proportion to my misdoing. Let this be a lesson to all rebellious wives; but poor comfort to me. . . .

They say; that horrible they, who are they? They say confession is a great relief, as liberating and loosening as a flood of tears, to the confessor. I don't agree—I find it unmitigatedly painful; a rough-going gallop that leaves me limp and extended.

And how is it that this "they" embodies the worst instincts of the community: of petty persecution? I am a permanent victim of their spite, because I do openly what they do in hiding; there is no worse sin to them than the flouting of conventions; what is not seen does not exist.

Does the perversity of my nature now dare complain that: —having carefully and methodically cut off all family ties, deliberately antagonized friends; and made myself generally as intractable, offensive, violent, and as similar to an infuriated wild boar from the horniest jungle as I know, and that is something I do know about—that I am ostracized? It does. That I have no friends? It does. That nobody loves me? It does. Can insanity go further than that? All for the sake of the mythical, majestic, mountainous furrow I am supposed to be ploughing in my little stagnant ditch of endeavour.

Then when I get a good old-fashioned kick in the teeth, the first thing I do is start snivelling for friends, blubbering and puking for mother; and all the distant, dimly remembered, soothing comforters of my indignantly shunned past. Every bone in my body aches individually with a dragging weariness of pain, and the joints cry aloud for a warm balm; honeyed oil, to be poured, engulfing me, into the rusty sockets. Soporifics, drugs, nectars, elixirs, etc., I want them all; anything to transform me, to make me different, to forget myself even for a second.

But they only make me worse afterwards, when I come to, marooned on an island of reverberating drink; untouchable, unclean as a leper with my little bell of pain, which tinkles so intently with the insistence of an alarm on waking.

He said he loved me; that I was the only woman for him; and, whatever the evidence to the contrary, I believed him, and still do; and I am grateful for that important bit of faith. There is, happily, no limit to the faith of human nature in believing what it wants to believe. But the sudden removal of such a love, such a special love, on such an immortal scale, and the only one, was bound to cause a dropping out of the bottom of my all-in-Dylan world. . . .

Had I gone away, as I intended, I could have preserved my reputation of pride and dignity: of the "perfect Lady," their highest term of praise. . . . But, it was very odd, try as I would, I did not fit the role. There was something abnormally wrong with me. So instead I went to the opposite extreme, I did all the things a Lady should not do, and showed them, aggressively, just how unladylike a Lady can be. I gave myself up with selfless abandonment to being awful. I wallowed in excess; an excess of bodily surfeiting, to kill the critically carping maiden aunt of a mind that nagged the prostrate soul out of me. I sought filthily to purge the blood-thronging devils out of me by using the devil's own filthier-still instruments.

I stole their sons and husbands, doing violence to both our diversely raw feelings; violating purposefully my most precious holy vows to Dylan; saying his golden endearing words for me to them, making the same familiar sweet affectionate gestures; ruthlessly pillaging the long years of our woven heart together; inciting a deliberate sacrilege, a shameful sacrifice of our love that was too stubborn to be put out.

And all this fervour of destruction, to no, not one, flickering twinge of improvement, curative effect in my buried, unremitting black burning world; the ridiculous reverse: an increase in my inescapable dedication to Dylan and a mutilated guilt-soaked, pride-stripped body.

But the more they castigated, reviled and morally spat on me; they would gleefully have tarred and feathered me, and with screams of ecstasy, set light to me in the market square; the more I persisted in scandalizing them. Had they offered a grain of sympathy, a nod or a touch of understanding, it would have been my undoing: my tough, dissembling, distended-to-breaking-point guts, would have melted in a weak pool at their gracious feet. As it was, I managed to preserve, with admirable conviction; sometimes, I asked myself, was it true or was it not, because what one does with enough will, one may very well become; the impossible myth of the monstrous scarlet woman, till my eventual, bridge of wives, windily sighing with relief, departure.

"If only," they whispered, and hissed in kitchen corners and back room bars malignantly, their bridling better-than-thou-ness glowing reassuringly in their wilting bird-caged breasts; "*she* could have waited a decent anonymity of years."

Years; did you hear that; how much time do they think I have, and how do they propose that I should kill that deposited squeamishly out-of-sight shelf of years? If I waited a million years, I could not forget Dylan: he will not come blundering down the path again, all misshapen, bulgy lumpy shapes, his loaded head rolling with old unforgettable poems and growing miracles of tomorrow singing, stifled, out of them; his pockets sagging with bottles and goodies, and bang at the door impatiently and shout, "Cait, come down quick and let me in." There will be nobody to bang at the door for he is in already.

But though I claimed to despise the morons, yet I minded terribly their unfriendliness, and was dying for a dram of kindness. I had given so much of myself to this God-forsaken, Dylan-shared, vanishing dip in the hills; much more than Dylan, who was so good at *containing* himself; that their turning on me and, metaphorically, stoning me out, made me feel like the most unjustly abused martyr.

The churchyard was always present to me, in that worst of awful periods, as an uncannily unbelievable place which, with all my elaborate deviations, I could never avoid landing up at; drawn by Dylan's rotting remains. And I would try to envisage how much was left of him; how much had started to crumble; and an impotent rage against the vile crudeness of nature daring to infringe on him, of all people, made me long to tear open that shoddy grey, speechless mound; ferret down to the long locked cold box, and burst it apart. There to press my headlong hot flesh into his, to mangle him with my strong bones, mingle, mutilate the two of us together, till the dead and the living would be desired One.

But instead I stood immovable, as near as possible without being seen, for I was ashamed to show myself in that conventional abode of lawful grief, and wept invisibly. And "they" said: "It is too much trouble for *her* to put a jampot of flowers on the grave."

Dorothy Livesay

Widow

No longer any man needs me
nor is the dark night of love
coupled

But the body is relentless, knows
its need
must satisfy itself without the seed
must shake in dreams, fly up the stairs
backwards.

In the open box in the attic
a head lies, set sideways.

This head from this body is severed.

Carolyn Kizer

A Widow in Wintertime

Last night a baby gargled in the throes
Of a fatal spasm. My children are all grown
Past infant strangles; so, reassured, I knew
Some other baby perished in the snow.
But no. The cat was making love again.

Later, I went down and let her in.
She hung her tail, flagging from her sins.
Though she'd eaten, I forked out another dinner,
Being myself hungry all ways, and thin
From metaphysic famines she knows nothing of,

The feckless beast! Even so, resemblances
Were on my mind: female and feline, though
She preens herself from satisfaction, and does
Not mind lying even in snow. She is
Loftly and bedraggled, without need to choose.

As an ex-animal, I look fondly on
Her excesses and simplicities, and would not return
To them; taking no marks for what I have become,
Merely that my nine lives peal in my ears again
And again, ring in these austerities,

These arbitrary disciplines of mine,
Most of them trivial: like covering
The children on my way to bed, and trying
To live well enough alone, and not to dream
Of grappling in the snow, claws plunged in fur,

Or waken in a caterwaul of dying.

Richard Meryman

from *Hope: A Loss Survived*

Once Hope was buried, I could collapse into the numbness
that marks the first phase of mourning. Because I was anesthe-
tized by shock, nothing had palpable existence for me except
the children and the Dublin house and the New Hampshire
countryside. I was faking my way through the days, playing
along by ear, riding the rhythms around me. There was, however, a subtle euphoria in this half-life—like the release and
extravagance of a vacation. I distracted myself with the children,
sledding, tobogganing, and skiing. The three of us needed
physical challenges that demanded strength and concentration,

and replaced restlessness with muscular fatigue—intense, minute-to-minute realities that were unconnected to Hope, to the big reality of her death.

But the fundamental weight of grief is unshakable. I was careful about anything, including alcohol and mention of Hope's death, that would weaken control of my emotions. The children, too, seemed to avoid whatever might rub on fragile feelings— steering clear of their Aunt Lanie as though worried she might play the substitute mother. In this stunned, brittle state, the three of us asked for what we wanted—without asking. The children came unbidden to my lap, to Charlotte's and Laura's, and received our calm hugs and ran away reassured. Reading our needs, hiding the thoughts that underpinned everything, the entire household maintained a festive mood, in itself a message of comfort and affection. But the bereaved do want recognition of their special status and their loss. Old family friends, Janet and Raleigh Hansl, arrived from Washington, D.C., and Janet caught me alone and said, "Dick, I must tell you how we feel."

I cut her off, saying, "You don't have to tell me. I know." But I required that signal from her.

Meredith found Janet alone and said, "Did you know my mother died?"

"Yes, Mere, I do know it," Janet said.

Meredith, satisfied, turned quickly away.

Though I kept a space of privacy between me and others, I hungered for the intimate, tender support system so easily available to the children. A widower needs a wholly receiving audience for his endless ramblings of fear and sorrow. As much as a child he needs physical contact to comfort his tears and counteract his aloneness. The subtraction of his wife alters his identity, and he needs his self-esteem restored. He needs to sense an escape route out of anxiety and pain. He needs somebody entirely focused on him. The bereaved who have such a person do recover faster.

Married friends and relatives are usually absorbed in their

own full lives and heavy concerns. A single woman will give that needed time and intensity, and it is easy to see why many widowers make new connections quickly. In fact, half of all widowers remarry within eighteen months. For me Elizabeth Hauser was heaven-sent. She was simultaneously a link to the past and bridge to the future. Having been part of my agony for months, she exactly understood my feelings. I called her daily from Dublin, reaching, clutching, pouring out my quandaries and incoherent emotions, and I invariably asked anxiously, "You are coming up, aren't you?"

We discussed her decision at length. Liz cared about conventional mores, about the decency of a single woman materializing now at my side. But she intensely identified the anguish of my bereavement with the trauma of her divorce. By nature impetuous and almost compulsively helpful, she could not resist my need and her empathy. Also, she had been profoundly involved with both Hope and me, and was, I think, caught up in the momentum, perhaps even the romance, of my drama.

I knew that the sudden surfacing of Liz was inappropriate. The behavior of the bereaved is prescribed: a subdued demeanor, a quiet life, a seemly interval of seclusion. But actually, the interval since Hope's death seemed vast to me. The visit did not feel premature. Time elapses differently for the bereaved. It creeps. Every minute had been so fraught, so filled with emotions, events and high drama, that each day had passed like a week.

Moreover, in the first days and months of mourning, there was an animal sense of self-preservation that brushed aside propriety and permitted whatever gave relief. In my dazed condition, disconnected from sober realities—somewhat crazy from shock— I told myself that I had earned the right to be selfish, that after giving for so long, the time had come to take. I did not truly care what people thought. I did not care if I was exploiting and manipulating Liz. I did not care about the problems I might be setting up in the future. I did not care about caution and good sense. I wanted to get well.

I guiltily did a selling job on Harry and Lanie, extolling Liz's friendship for Hope, her long history of help to Hope, her closeness to the children, her warm and comforting qualities. I also had to tell the children. During mourning, the ancient contest of will between parent and child is even more equal, the parent is depleted and the bereaved child wields the power of pathos.

Meredith said, "Fine" with clear, almost disinterested eyes, but I knew she was luxuriating in the full attention of Laura, Charlotte, and Harry's older daughter, Louise. Helena, however, was clinging to me—taking me away for her closed-door talks, riding the sled and the ski lift with me, sitting beside me at meals, climbing into bed with me at night—already putting me into Hope's place. She had now transferred to me the double hand squeeze that meant "I love you," and she would do it surreptitiously—each time breaking my heart. When I told her about Liz, she said angrily, "Why does *she* have to come?"

"Because I'm like you," I said. "I'm very unhappy. And it would be nice for me to have somebody here to talk to who has been a good friend to me and Mommy."

"We talk."

"That's true. I would be ten times sadder without you and Mere. But adults need adults, and I want to keep on being your daddy who takes care of you—and that won't change because Liz is here." I thought to myself, half apologetically, that if Helena planned to take me over, perhaps it was just as well if a Liz Hauser entered now.

On New Year's Day, leaving the children in the lavish care of the three older girls, I drove to the Keene airport to meet Liz. I was very nervous. Stricken once again by my boyhood insecurities with women, I was frightened that I was entrapping myself in a rash commitment, but the fear only magnified a romantic sense of inevitability. In the muddle of my emotions, my mind felt no more in charge of this turn of my life than in control of Hope's death.

Liz appeared in the entrance gate, tall, slender, a fur parka framing a silver and turquoise Zuñi necklace, dark hair, dramatic, olive-skinned face, eyes very bright. The sympathetic voice on the telephone was now a woman separate from Hope's illness. I felt that I hardly knew her. I was stiff and self-conscious as we talked blandly about her trip. In the car I reached for her, feeling that I was throwing myself through a barrier of inhibition. I held her very hard and we kissed and raw emotion erupted inside me and I groaned—a miniature cataclysm, a first momentous severance from Hope. It was a reach for a person able to mitigate my needs *now*. I said, "Oh, Liz, I'm so glad you're here."

At the house in Dublin the entire group was assembled before dinner in the living room, waiting for that awkward, comic moment which must happen to every widower—the arrival of a new and unknown woman. From my apologetic description of this adored friend of Hope's, they expected a comfortable, commodious auntie, buxom and bubbly—a Gotham earth mother. Now before their gaze stood an Indian queen.

The mood was festive, even cheerfully raucous, and I soon began to feel lighter, less alone. I was satisfying that impulse to return to the old status quo and reenter the normal world. But there was nothing normal about those days. I was on a shock high, careening along quite free of reality, winging Liz along with me. That night, as usual, I slept fitfully and woke at dawn. The sky was clear, the air still. I gently opened Liz's door and sat on the edge of her bed. She woke and looked up at me, startled but glad. I bent down and kissed her and buried my face in the pillow, my cheek next to hers. Her arms came around me, and I was filled with a simultaneous calm and excitement. There were no overtones of passion. So complex was this connection that the limit of my desire was to hold and be held. "Right now before anybody is up," I said, "let's go for a walk on the lake."

Warm in snow boots and parkas, we slipped from the house. I was reminded fleetingly of that long-ago departure for Spain, though the vast compartment of Hope was shut away and I existed only in this small moment. A few hundred yards down a forest-bordered road was Dublin Lake, a prairie of unbroken snow. Rising up on the far side was Mount Monadnock, a single, glorious peak of granite and gleaming ice. Gripping each other's arm, we forged out into that vast white space. I was intoxicated —by a feeling of mastery as this woman clutched me; by a sensation of newness as though we were pre-teens trying our first, tentative, thrilling intimacy; by the exhilaration of cold and brilliant sun; by the familiar landscape awesome and romantic under the snow.

Weaving through our excitement, and supercharging it, were the currents of anguish and pity and the strangeness of Liz here in this way. I began talking compulsively about Hope, saying it was important for me and the children that I be honest about her, that I not glorify her into a dream deity that no future woman could match. I told Liz, "It wasn't easy living with Hopie." As I went on to describe her temper, my loss overwhelmed me and I began to cry. Liz held me and then we moved on, spirited again as I pointed out houses on the hills and told their histories. Then, in the middle of the lake, centered in that vast, frozen void, we stopped and kissed and I remember the startling warmth of Liz's face. Isolated from everything—in a sense from ourselves—we were riding an illusionary crescendo. Romance is a route out of grief, but this form of romance was cool filaments wrapping and soothing the fearful heat of grief.

Mary Jane Moffat

Widow's Supper

Her fork clinks
against obdurate china
and a certain conversation begins.

Through the blowing curtain
the late sun presents
movement and shade
to the cloth, the cutlery,
the single plate.

Knife cuts chicken,
yellow juice flows,
someone absent
asks for the salt.

She nods and the napkin
pressed to her lips
accepts the small stories
of the day. A gossip
stones must exchange
when they're alone.

Frederic Lawrence Knowles
1869–1905

from Grief and Joy

Joy is a partnership,
  Grief weeps alone;
Many guests had Cana,
  Gethsemane had one.

Anne Philipe

The widow of French film actor Gérard Philipe, Anne Philipe
kept a journal after his death in 1959.

---

from *No Longer Than a Sigh*

I must admit that for the first time memories invade me. I call
them up, I ask their help to live. I come back to myself and
forage in the past. Sometimes I resent you for being dead. You
have deserted me, left me. . . .

I no longer look for your face. For a long time you sprang
up everywhere. How to find a path, a street, a quay that we
haven't explored together? I had either to flee or to brave all
these places alone. In the many faces of the crowd or in the
solitude of a woodland path I saw nothing but your face. My
reason refused these mirages, but my heart searched them out.
You were both absent and present. Every hour I questioned myself: how is it possible that I live—not that I live, but simply
that my heart continued to beat now that yours has stopped? I
sometimes heard it said that you are present among us. I agreed.
What good would it do to deny it? I told myself that it is easy
for some to accept death. Are they trying to reassure themselves
of their own eternity? . . .

I still find it difficult to live in the present; I rarely cling to
it without effort. When we used to speak of death, we thought
that the worst would be for one of us to survive the other. I
don't know any longer. I search, and the reply varies depending
on the day. When I am seized by the throat by the grace of spring,
or when I watch our children—each time I am touched by the
beauty of life and for an instant am overjoyed by it without
thinking of you (for your absence never lasts longer than an
instant)—I realize that you, not I, bear the sacrifice. But when I
an ensnared by my pain, diminished and humiliated by my pain,
I tell myself that we were right and that dying is a small thing. I

contradict myself incessantly. I want and don't want to suffer by your absence. When the anguish seems most inhuman and appears to have no possible end, I want to be relieved, but each time you leave me a little repose I refuse to lose contact, to let our last days and last sight of each other grow blurred for the price of a certain serenity, and a love of life catches me up again almost unbeknownst to me. And thus, without ever finding repose, and without stopping, I balance from one extreme to the other before I find an equilibrium that is menaced incessantly.

It will be like this for a long time. I know it. But sometimes an immense fatigue overwhelms me, and a terrible temptation invades me. I want to rest, to lay down arms. I love the earth at these moments, and the idea of going to sleep in it, half marmot and half statue, frightens me not at all. At these moments I do not imagine the decay that sometimes obsesses me; I simply contemplate a natural disintegration that has nothing of the frightening. . . .

Perhaps I am saved today? I don't know. The past absorbs me, and I lead the present to it. Yet the business of living continues to be accomplished in me. I know it, I want it that way, and yet I know as clearly as can be that these are the shadows of days. . . . When I go out in the evening, I leave the light on. When I come back I see it shine behind the curtains and I smile at myself, at my ineffectual ruses, for as soon as I have opened the door my solitude bursts upon me like a gust of wind. I open and close the closets, I move bottles, I turn faucets, but I hear only silence and your absence. I listen to it; it does not frighten me, it fascinates me. I have no desire to interrupt it. Sleep will come; as it has come for hundreds of nights while I listened to your absence.

On certain days the reality of you escapes me. Did that joy and that beauty really exist? Were they part of my daily life? Then my thought seems to come unstuck, and it wafts above the past, avoiding its asperities, and becomes disincarnate. I am left holding only a dream and ashes, what was slips away, and suddenly I discover how the process of idealization I've heard mentioned comes about. There is that complacent part of memory which, little by little, schematizes and takes the place of truth. It is an easy treason when reality is no longer there to contradict the gentle image that forms in the spirit. . . .

Nothing is more serious than the conversation of children. They dare question the primordial things to find solutions; they go to the very heart of the matter. We often talked about death with them. I did not know then that it would brush so close by them so soon. "He's dead, he's asleep," they would say of the grasshoppers and lizards they sometimes found around the house. No problem. But all that would change.

A few months later they would discover the meaning of "never again," and the one that suffered the most, being best able to measure its significance, said to me one day, speaking of you: "Well, get me another if that one's dead. I want another just like him."

I tried to explain—explain what? That love. . .

"But you can't love somebody who's dead, since you'll never see him again," was the reply.

"And where is he now? Can he see us?"

"No, I don't think he can see us. But we can see him in our memory."

"I have his eyes and his mouth, don't I?"—proudly.

"And I move just the way he used to?" said the other.

"That's true."

"But his body—where did you bury it?"

I answered, on the hill. I couldn't bring myself to say, in the cemetery. I would have wanted you to be without a coffin, just simply alone at the foot of one of our trees. There, where we liked to take walks. Why are all our rituals so lugubrious and unnatural? The funerals on the banks of the Ganges don't do away with pain, which everyone must deal with as best he can; but they don't try to express it in some outside fashion. I wanted our children to keep a luminous vision of you, and never be touched by that idea of the putrefaction of the body which pursued me for months. I could never admit that your grace and beauty could turn into some repulsive thing. I followed the decomposition of your body; it haunted me. I kept telling myself that it was nothing, that you knew nothing about it, it was a chemical phenomenon; but then I would see your body, your eyes and your lips and the material of your suit, and when somebody said to a child afraid of a wasp or a fly in my presence, "Little animals don't eat big animals," I thought: Yes they do, that's just it, they do; to the last mouthful. Yes, I wanted to keep all that to myself, but I didn't want to say either that you were in the sky, since that's not what we believed. So I tried to link you with life. I said, he's been transformed, he has become two trees and some flowers. Bees crawl inside the flowers and make honey, and we eat the honey and that way everything begins all over.

Each reacted according to his nature:

"He was so handsome," said one of them. "He must have made marvelous flowers!"

The other thought in silence and came to me next day.

"You mean, each time we eat honey we eat a little of someone?" ...

I see in them resemblances that delight and touch me. They are often elusive, traveling from one to the other. Suddenly there is a gesture, a way of lacing a shoe, of liking the same hours, the same skies, a way of waking up in the morning or a glance I have never seen before. It may have existed before, but now I seem to see it being born. I listen and contemplate.

This way I follow the course of your life, and discover you at an age when I never knew you. I try to join these pictures they give me with that of you aged twenty, and so I perfect my knowledge of you.

I write, and it seems as if I were pulling apart an endless skein of yarn. The thread I follow leads me to you; it's not as

though I were advancing through a labyrinth, but as if I were
following the spirals of a sea shell. I am trying to arrive at the
heart of what we were. When I think I have reached it, I
realize it is only yet another stage. I must go still farther, travel
the space of other remembrance and sensation, rid myself of a kind
of envelope each time, and only so will I arrive at the place I
think is there and want to arrive at. I am the only one to know
my victories and defeats. Sometimes I think I'm going forward
and I feel at peace with myself, and then, all of a sudden, there's
nothing left; no backbone, no flesh, some acid has dissolved it
all and the thread is severed; I am a little formless spot where a
few nerves contract vainly.

There is nothing to be gained by face-to-face battle. You
need diversive action, what people call distraction; the things
that usually fill me with horror. I leave and I walk, without
thinking about anything, fleeing before myself. I need air on my
face and solid ground under my feet. To forget everything, to be
empty. When I feel my fatigue I am almost saved. I exist. I come
back to earth. And I am astonished to find everything in its
accustomed place. . . .

I don't really remember the day I first felt that all was not
irremediably lost. Was it a child's smile that awoke me, or a sign
of sadness exposed in a place I didn't want it seen? Or a sense of
responsibility? Or had I finally used up despair? Perhaps I was
simply caught up again in the game of life. The truth has so
many facets that it is impossible for me to say exactly how I
regained my footing. One day I became aware that I had stopped
being only a façade. I existed, I breathed. I wanted once again
to act on the events of the world. Slowly I took stock and ex-
amined what remained of me. It was at that moment that I
stopped suffering solitude and started to allow myself to be won
over by it.

Now it has become familiar, we know each other well, and
I can look it in the eye. I talk of it with friends who have always
taken it for granted. For me there is no finer sight in the world

than a couple, and when I hear someone say that loving means losing your liberty and integrity I wonder whether he's speaking of the same emotion that I know.

One evening I was leafing through a book and my eye fell on a piece of sculpture we had often looked at together; a woman's body strung like a cry of joy between earth and sky. I sat there, staring at it in a daze, but I didn't turn the page. Images of the past rose up and I saw a sort of endless movie and heard a song of victory: then both were broken into by a November day. I felt as though I were climbing out of a sucking marsh. I was alone in my room, but I was filling it completely; it seemed different from the way it had been on the other days. I had somehow gone back into gear. I was able once again to contemplate beauty.

And yet everything still hurt, and above all those looks that couples exchange, their kind of collusion above the heads of the crowd; a wink and it was as if two birds had come together and were taking flight over all those voices and cigarette smoke and whisky. There was the summit of existence; their meeting had put the world back in focus and life was once more what it should be. Then it doesn't matter what one hears or says, the birds are there, they are watching over us, and soon, in the street, we shall see them again. For me those two birds are dead, but I remain sensitive to the whir of other wings, and I know without fail when they are present. Actually, I am always astonished that they seem so rare. . . .

The day of your burial, when I left the cemetery, I knew I would go back there often. I might have been the same, loved you just as much, and never have gone back again. That first evening, as I closed my shutters, I glimpsed the moonless sky, stifling and immense. I was alone on earth. The clouds scudded by; I should have wanted them to take me with them. I drew my curtains as an animal goes to earth in its lair. I would never be able to look at the sky again, nor at anything I loved. How would I be able to stand the sight of my children? For three days I had not thought of them.

The next day I went to find you. A mad rendezvous, and one more monologue. I remained outside reality, without being able to go in. The tomb was there, I could touch the earth that covered you, and without being able to help it, I began to believe that you would come, a little late as usual; that soon I would feel you approach me, that we would gaze together on this tomb just barely closed up.

There was no point in telling myself that you were dead, the illusion was beginning again. You weren't coming, no, you were waiting for me in the car. A mad hope, that I knew to be mad, and still it overtook me.

"Yes, he's waiting in the car." And, when I found it empty, I protected myself once more, as though trying to give myself respite: "He's taking a walk on the hill." I went down to the house, talking to friends the while, looking for you on the road. Without believing in it, of course.

That evening I went back to Paris. It seemed to me as though I were abandoning you. . . .

I went back to the house the next summer. My first vacation without you. I had left Paris in a sweltering heat; and from dawn on I watched the hills and cypresses and vineyards swing by, and then the sea, which seemed to grow out of a mist barely different from the sky. I saw once again that absence of color and that shimmer of light, and I understood something I hadn't admitted to myself—that I was preparing myself for another meeting, and that this unconscious thought had decided my return. All the now familiar contradictions arose once more: to flee you or to seek you out, to make a meeting place of the cemetery or say and believe that from now you were alive only in my memories and in our children. In spite of all reason, I went to meet an image of you that I knew no longer existed, that last, before the men in black enshrouded you in thin linen and lead weights. I walked toward you, toward the two trees and the border of stones. What could I hope for? ...

The trees had grown taller and the soil had sunk. I used to believe in the peace of cemeteries. We liked to pay our respects to the tombs of Van Gogh and Theo at Auvers. We liked the ivy that covered them, and told each other that a cemetery is a calm and serene place, that it is good to go home and feel the warmth of the fire at the end of day when there are two to watch the growing moon, listen to the owls, and listen, in confidence, to the silence. But that day, standing before you, the sky blue and the cypresses almost black, the delicate breeze was only a décor. I was possessed by the thought of hidden things, that inhuman and subterranean life where we all decay alone, you as the others, only a yard from my eyes.

How many years would it take, probably several hundred, for the simple matter that makes up a human body to be integrated into the layers of ground and become dust, the salt of the earth, a few handfuls of sand some future man would lift and run through his fingers, as we had liked to do, our eyes closed, our bodies stretched out facing the sun, our arms spread wide, while our hands played hourglass, noticing the fineness of the sand and its soft, living heat.

I imagined the millions of cells assembled to make up a beloved being like a rain of stars that would never repeat itself in exactly this form again. Then, suddenly, I felt myself grow reasonable. There was no meeting. I was alone before you, dead, alone facing the void. I could resuscitate your voice or relisten to our conversations, I could see your movements and I could also invent a present, establish an imaginary dialogue; but in truth there was nothing to be expected of you. This was the reality. You were absent from the world forever. A merciless little voice that I know well repeated: "Live or die; but decide. You have to choose." ...

Months, years pass, and the seasons change. Now there is a new spring. In the still air I feel it come to me in gusts. It gives and takes away strength and hope. Subtle or heavy, it insinuates itself into the marrow of my bones. It needs only a patch of spring, the suddenly warmer air, a bird's song or a bursting bud on the tree in my courtyard—or even the sound of rain, or laughter outside my window—for all to be in question once more. The calm I thought I had acquired, the wisdom I was so proud of, my resolutions, reality accepted, revolt put down, pain dampened—suddenly my finest strongholds have crumbled to sand. Suddenly the typhoon is here; it has simply been lying in wait, ready to pounce upon me with the first gentle sky or the first green shoots that make a fragile halo around the head of a tree.

"It's spring, I'm going to wear white socks. All my friends are wearing them," my daughter says.

Yes, the animal is alive; it scents, it knows, it intuits rightly. My reason notes relations of cause and effect but cannot keep me from trembling. The body never lies, it knows how to call for order. I feel limp, invaded by fatigue. Then I come out of my torpor to go from rage to pain. It is simply scandalous for you not to be here. . . .

Spring hurts. I would like to ask it to spare me. Every year I hope I will be ready to live or that I will have forgotten its savor. Have I not gone a step ahead? Am I like a squirrel caged on a wheel? Could I have rolled myself in a ball at the bottom of my bed since the day of your death and not be any worse off?

The warm air makes me dream of what was, and of what would be if you were here. I know that this dream is but an inaptitude to live the present. I allow myself to drift on this current without looking too far or too deep. I await the moment when I will find my strength again. It will come. I know that life still fascinates me. I want to save myself, not deliver myself from you.

Translated from the French by Cornelia Schaeffer

Antonio Machado
1875–1939

Machado's poems to his wife Leonor are considered to be among the best of twentieth-century Spanish poetry.

---

from *The Dream Below the Sun*

ROADS

From the Moorish city
behind the old ramparts,
I study the silent afternoon,
alone with my shadow and my grief.

The river is running
between shaded orchards
and gray olive groves,
through the happy fields of Baeza.

The vines have golden tendrils
over red stalks.
Guadalquivir, like a broken scattered cutlass,
glitters and mirrors.

Far, the mountains sleep
wrapped in haze,
maternal autumn haze; the soft rues
rest from their lives in stone
on this warm November afternoon,
pious, mauve, violet.

Wind has shaken
the musty elms of the highway,
raising the dust of the land

in pink whirlwinds.
The moon is rising and full.

The small white roads
cross and move away,
seeking the scattered villages
of the valley and the sierra.
Roads in the fields.
O, but now I cannot walk with her!

———

Lord, what I loved the most you tore from me.
Now hear again this heart cry out alone.
Your will was done, O Lord, against my own.
Lord, we're alone now, my heart and the sea.

———

There in the highlands
where the Duero draws
its crossbow curve
around Soria, between leaden hills
and stains of wasted oaks,
my heart is wandering, in dreams . . .

"Leonor, do you see the river aspens
with their firm foliage?
Look at blue and white Moncayo, give me
your hand and let us walk."
Through the fields of my land,
edged with dusty olive trees,
I am walking alone,
sad, tired, pensive and old.

———

I dreamed you led me
along a white footpath

through green fields
toward the blue of the sierras,
toward the blue mountain
one serene morning.

I felt your hand in mine,
your companion hand,
your child's voice in my ear
like a new bell,
the pristine bell
of a spring dawn.
It was your voice and hand
in dreams, so true!
Live, hope, who knows
what the earth devours!

Translated from the Spanish by Willis Barnstone

Lily Pincus

Lily Pincus is an English social worker and a founder of the Institute for Marital Studies at the Tavistock Institute for Human Relations in London. After eleven years of widowhood, at the age of seventy-five, she wrote *Death and the Family: The Importance of Mourning*, based largely on case studies of couples who came to her for counseling. She begins with some personal memories of her reactions to the death of her husband, Fritz, after a lingering illness.

Personal Memories

For a few days before Fritz's cremation I stayed in my brother's house where I was supported and cared for with all tenderness.

This was a great comfort, but I was restless and longing to be in my home—our home. Yet when I put the key into the apartment door I had a moment of panic and stood hesitatingly on the doorstep, until I felt clearly a "Welcome home" emanating from inside. The sun was shining and a neighbor, who had heard me come in, called out to offer a cup of tea. In spite of the emptiness and the sense of desolation, it was a homecoming and the beginning of a new life.

Through the first days and weeks, my family, friends, neighbors, and colleagues showed me love and sympathy. They left me alone, and yet were there whenever and for whatever I wanted them. A young male colleague with my husband's build came with suitcases within the first week and emptied wardrobes and drawers. For many years I enjoyed encounters with Fritz's clothes on him, and even now, ten years later, I still recognize sometimes with a pang of pleasure a familiar tie.

But in spite of all the affection and care, I was often depressed and lonely, however much I tried to apply to the situation of bereavement what I had learned from Fritz's dying. I knew that here too the full acceptance of the finality of loss, and all the pain that goes with it, need not diminish life but could give it a new quality of fulfillment. I also knew that this could not be achieved without going through the agonies of grief and mourning. I had had eleven years of expecting this loss, which should have given me the opportunity for anticipatory mourning —and I had deceived myself into believing that I had used this opportunity in spite of my conscious chief concern, which had been to support Fritz in his dying. I had often been puzzled by statements in studies about bereavement that the severity of grief may not be lessened by years of anticipating loss, but quite the contrary, may even be more severe than in the case of sudden death. Now, thinking about my own experience, I am beginning to understand that if so much of one's life for many years has been absorbed by the joint task of facing death, sharing it with the dying person by complete involvement, then one's own feelings may have to be almost completely obliterated in order not to deprive both partners of the possibilities still remaining in the relationship. In these circumstances the healthy partner has to remove himself so much from living experience that it may be difficult to be sufficiently in touch with himself to experience his own feelings of anticipatory mourning. In this sense, the shock of an unexpected death can be easier to cope with than a long-prepared-for loss.

An additional strain, connected with Fritz's long illness, and one others in my situation have shared, was my inability for two or three years to recall him as he was before he got ill. I remember lying awake at night, struggling in vain to recapture his image. All my visual memories were of the emaciated, suffering Fritz, a beautiful image but not that of the man with whom I had spent and enjoyed such a large part of my life. How much I suffered through this blockage I only realized fully through the ecstasy of joy and relief when finally I could again recall the younger, healthy Fritz.

After the first few days of exhaustion and numbness, of a degree of confusion which made living a virtually insurmountable task (I lost and mislaid everything and got myself into the most painful situations), I went back to work. My job was to help people with their problems, mostly marital, and although I understood the roots of their lack of mutual tolerance and their often childish, unrealistic demands on each other, I found that the work with them was a great strain at the moment when my own marriage had just so sadly ended.

It began to dawn on me that now, as before, I was using my concern for others to avoid facing my own pain and loss. I had even gone to the Clinic on the evening after Fritz's death to see a man who had been particularly distressed at our previous meeting and who I felt could not stand the strain of a missed session.

This "good deed" and my growing physical exhaustion helped to convince me that I needed to get away from my commitments, to give up being in the helping role, to have time for myself and my grief. I was therefore glad to accept an invitation to go to Israel for three months and give lectures and seminars on "Marital Interaction as a Focus for Casework" at the Hebrew University and various other institutions.

On my way there I planned to stay for a week in Zurich with a dear friend of Fritz's and mine, a beautiful woman, full of energy, health, and vitality, who had shared much of our lives. Within an hour of receiving a letter from her with plans for our time together, a telegram arrived with the news that she had electrocuted herself through a faulty appliance in the bathroom. This news completely overwhelmed me; it was as if my carefully maintained defenses against breaking down could not withstand the shock. I collapsed helplessly and then did all the crying, expressed all the grief which really belonged to the loss of my husband. After a few days I did what I was expected to do, "I pulled myself together." This did not seem to be the time for mourning. I was on the eve of departure to a new land, exciting new impressions, pressing new demands. That I managed to fracture my ankle within ten days of my arrival in Israel and was forced to rest, may indicate, however, that I had learned something from my previous attempts at avoiding grief. When I asked the orthopedic surgeon who treated me whether people often fracture bones after bereavement, he said, without even looking up from my injured foot, "Naturally, people lose their sense of balance," and perhaps some have to fracture limbs or hurt some other part of themselves before they can acknowledge what has happened to them. Is it possible to enable them to do so in a less self-destructive way, by encouraging and supporting them in their mourning process?

Daphne du Maurier

Death and Widowhood

Death, to the novelist, is a familiar theme. Often it is the high spot of a particular tale, turning romance to tragedy. A character, his demise planned for a certain chapter while the story was still in notebook form, vanishes from the manuscript, and the author, like a successful murderer whose victim has disappeared, decides that the killing was well done. I have done this several times in my novels. I can even confess I enjoyed the killing. It gave a certain zest to the writing, and if I felt an inward pang for the loss of the character I had created, the pang was soon forgotten and the memory faded. The fictitious person was, after all, only a puppet of my imagination, and I could create others to take his place. The writer, like a spider, spins a web; the creatures caught in the web have no substance, no reality.

It is only when death touches the writer in real life that he, or she, realises the full impact of its meaning. The deathbed scene, described so often in the past, with fingers tapping it out upon a typewriter or pen scratching it on paper, becomes suddenly true. The shock is profound. Sometimes this encounter with reality can so awaken the writer from the imaginary world that he never recovers. I believe that this is what happened to Emily Brontë. The fantasy world of Gondal that had been hers, peopled with heaven knows how many persons, coupled with the harsher, wilder land of Heathcliffe, Cathy and *Wuthering Heights*, faded on a certain Sunday morning when her brother Branwell, his dragging illness accepted with resignation for so long, of a sudden died. A cold, caught at his funeral and then neglected, hastened her own decline and death barely three months afterwards. It does not account for her stubborn refusal to see a doctor, her silence with her two sisters, her complete withdrawal within herself, which can only be explained by shock, or trauma as we would call it today, occasioned by direct experience of death. The death of a brother, for which she blamed her sisters and herself. They had neglected him. Therefore, she argued, she must be neglected likewise. It was an unconscious form of suicide, not uncommon to the suddenly bereaved.

I am a writer too. Neither a poet nor a great romantic novelist like Emily Brontë, but a spinner of webs, a weaver of imaginary tales; and when my husband died in March of this past year it was as though the sheltered cloudland that had enveloped me for years, peopled with images drawn from my imagination, suddenly dissolved, and I was face to face with a harsh and terrible reality. The husband I had loved and taken for granted for thirty-three years of married life, father of my three children, lay dead. If by writing about it now I expose myself and my feelings, it is not from a sense of self-advertisement, but because by doing so I may be able to help those readers who, like myself, have suffered the same sense of shock.

Like Emily Brontë, one of my first reactions, after the first bewildered fits of weeping, was to blame myself. I could have done more during the last illness, I should have observed, with sharp awareness, the ominous signs. I should have known, the last week, the last days, that his eyes followed me with greater intensity, and instead of moving about the house on trivial business, as I did, never left his side. How heartless, in retrospect, my last good night, when he murmured to me, "I can't sleep," and I kissed him and said, "You will, darling, you will," and went from the room. Perhaps, if I had sat with him all night, the morning would have been otherwise. As it was, when morning came, and the nurses who had shared his vigil expressed some anxiety about his pallor and asked me to telephone the doctor, I went through to him expecting possibly an increase of weakness, but inevitably the usual smile. Instead . . . he turned his face to me, and died.

My readers will have heard of the kiss of life. We tried it, the nurses and myself, in turn until the doctor came. But I knew, as I breathed into his body, that it was useless and he was dead. His eyes were open but the spark had gone. What had been living was no more. This, then, was the finality of death. Described by myself in books time without number. Experienced at last.

The aftermath of shock must alter the chemistry in the blood, for it forced me to action instead of to collapse. I had to telephone my children. Make arrangements. See that necessary things were done. These responses were automatic, numb. Part of my brain functioned, part of it seemed closed. The part of it that was automatic and dissociated from emotion ordered an immediate autopsy so that the doctor's first assessment of death by sudden coronary thrombosis could be verified. The part of it that was numb began to fuse with the emotions, every instinct urging me to perform those actions he would have wished carried out, the wording to *The Times* making clear that by his own request the cremation should be private, there would be no memorial service, instead his friends might send donations to the Security Fund for Airborne Forces—those Airborne Forces he had commanded in 1942, 1943 and 1944, his beloved "paras," his glider pilots.

It was not until the cremation was over, which only my children and a few close friends attended, and I had scattered my husband's ashes at the end of the garden where we often walked together, and my children had returned to their own homes, that I knew, with full force, the finality of death. I was alone. The newly discovered tenderness of my daughters, the sudden maturity of my son, himself to become a father within a few months, had not prevailed upon me to go back with one of them, to recover, as they put it, from the strain. "No," I told them. "I want to face the future here, in my own home, by myself." To go elsewhere, even with them, would postpone the moment of truth. What had to be endured must be endured now, and at once, alone.

In marriage one partner—unless both are killed simultaneously—must go before the other. Usually the man goes first. Generations of wives have known this. Now I knew it too, and must adapt. I must force myself to look upon the familiar things, the coat hanging on the chair, the hat in the hall, the motoring gloves, the stick, the pile of yachting magazines beside his bed, and remind myself that this was not the separation of war that we had known twenty years earlier, but separation for all time.

To ease the pain I took over some of his things for myself. I wore his shirts, sat at his writing desk, used his pens to acknowledge the hundreds of letters of condolence; and, by the very process of identification with the objects he had touched, felt the closer to him. The evenings were the hardest to bear. The ritual of the hot drink, the lumps of sugar for the two dogs, the saying of prayers—his boyhood habit carried on throughout our married life—the good night kiss. I continued the ritual, because this too lessened pain, and was, in its very poignancy, a consolation.

I wept often because I could not prevent the tears, and possibly, in some way beyond my understanding, tears helped the healing process, but the physical act of weeping was distressing to me beyond measure. As a child I seldom cried.

I thought long and often about the possibility of life after death. Baptised and confirmed in the Christian faith, I acknowledge no denomination, yet have an instinctive yearning for survival, as indeed the human race has always done, since man first sought to come to terms with death. I liked to think of my husband reunited with the parents who had gone before him, and with his comrades of two world wars. I liked to think that all pain, all suffering, had been wiped out, that he knew, as none of us can know here on earth, indescribable joy, the "peace which passes all understanding"—a line he used to quote.

Yet I had seen his empty shell. I had seen the light flicker and go out. Where had it gone? Was it blown to emptiness after all, like the light of a candle, and does each one of us, in the end, vanish into darkness? If this is so, and our dreams of survival after death are only dreams, then we must accept this too. Not with fear and dismay, but with courage. To have lived at all is a measure of immortality; for a baby to be born, to become a man, a woman, to beget others like himself, is an act of faith in itself, even an act of defiance. It is as though every human being born into this world burns, for a brief moment, like a star, and because of its pinpoint of light shines in the darkness, and so there is glory, so there is life. If there is nothing more than this, we have achieved our immortality.

Meanwhile, for the bereaved, who will never know the answer here on earth, the practical living of day-by-day continues. We must rise in the morning, eat, go about business, watch the seasons pass, our life no longer shared. To plan for one, instead of two, brings a sense of apathy. Instinct says, "Why bother? What can the future hold?" The sense of urgency is lacking. A younger woman, with a family to rear, would be spurred by necessity to action. The older woman has no such driving force. Her children are adult, they can fend for themselves. The older woman must seek her reason for living either in outward forms— good works, committees, the demanding tasks of a career—or look inward, deep within herself, for a new philosophy.

"At least," said a kind, well-wishing friend, "you have your writing," as though, with a magic wand, I could conjure at will a host of dancing puppets to grimace and do my bidding, their very antics proving an antidote to pain. Yes, I have my writing, but the stories that I fashioned once were fairy tales, and they cannot satisfy me now. Death, surely, will make me more aware of other people's suffering, of other people's ills, of the countless women there must be who, widowed like myself, have no form of consolation from without or from within. Some lack children, sisters, friends; others are financially bereft; a vast number lived in their husband's shadow, and with the shadow gone feel themselves not fully individuals, unwanted and ignored. What life can these women make for themselves, how will they adapt?

The widow, like the orphan, has been an object of pity from earliest times. She received charity. She lived, very often, with her married son or daughter, and earned, sometimes rightly, the hostility of her daughters- or sons-in-law. Her place was the chimney corner, and in more modern times the little flat upstairs or the bungalow next door.

The Hindu woman, in old days, committed suttee. She laid herself on the funeral pyre of her husband and was burnt with him. This was one way out of her dilemma. My own grandmother, widowed at the same age as myself, at fifty-eight, entered upon old age with grace and dignity. She donned her weeds and her widow's cap, and I can see her now, a kindly, grave, if rather formidable figure, endeavouring to teach me, a child, how to knit, in the First World War.

I look down today at my own weeds, dark slacks, a white pullover, and I wonder if the change in garb is basic, a symbol of woman's emancipation, or simply a newer fashion, while fundamentally the widow's sense of loss remains unchanged. No matter how brave a face she puts upon her status, the widow is still a lonely figure, belonging nowhere, resembling in some indefinable manner the coloured races in a world dominated by whites. The attitude of non-widowed is kindly, hearty, a little overcheerful in the attempt to show the bereaved that nothing is different, just as the liberal white will shake his black brother by the hand, smiling broadly, to emphasise equality. Neither is deceived. Both are embarrassed. The widow, aware of her inadequacy, retires into her shell, while the other, dreading the floodgates of emotion, beats a hasty retreat. Carried to extremes, the division results in apartheid, the widowed and the non-widowed withdraw to their separate worlds, and there is no communion between the two.

The old adage, Time heals all wounds, is only true if there is no suppuration within. To be bitter, to lament unceasingly, "Why did this have to happen to him?" makes the wound fester; the mind, renewing the stab, causes the wound to bleed afresh. It is hard, very hard, not to be bitter in the early days, not to blame doctors, hospitals, drugs, that failed to cure. Harder still for the woman whose husband died not by illness but by accident, who was cut short in full vigour, in the prime of life, killed perhaps in a car crash returning home from work. The first instinct is to seek revenge upon the occupants of the other car, themselves unhurt, whose selfish excess of speed caused the disaster. Yet this is no answer to grief. All anger, all reproach, turns inward upon itself. The infection spreads, pervading the mind and body.

I would say to those who mourn—and I can only speak from my own experience—look upon each day that comes as a challenge, as a test of courage. The pain will come in waves, some days worse than others, for no apparent reason. Accept the pain. Do not suppress it. Never attempt to hide grief from yourself. Little by little, just as the deaf, the blind, the handicapped develop with time an extra sense to balance disability, so the bereaved, the widowed, will find new strength, new vision, born of the very pain and loneliness which seem, at first, impossible to master. I address myself more especially to the middle-aged who, like myself, look back to over thirty years or more of married life and find it hardest to adapt. The young must, of their very nature, heal sooner than ourselves.

We know, and must face it honestly, that life for us can never be the same again. Marriage was not just another love affair, an episode, but the greater half of our existence. We can never give to another what we gave to the partner who has gone. All that is over, finished. And the years that lie ahead, ten, twenty, perhaps even thirty, must be travelled alone. This is a challenge, just as marriage, in the first place, was a challenge.

I remember on our wedding day, in July 1932, the good priest who married us drawing a comparison between the little boat in which we were to set forth on our honeymoon and marriage itself. "You will embark," he said, "on a fair sea, and at times there will be fair weather, but not always. You will meet storms and overcome them. You will take it in turns to steer your boat through fair weather and foul. Never lose courage. Safe harbour awaits you both in the end."

Today I remember this advice with gratitude. Even if I must, of necessity, steer my boat alone, I shall not, so I trust, lose my bearings but, because of all I have learnt through the past three-and-thirty years, with my fellow helmsman at my side, come eventually to my journey's end.

One final word to my contemporaries. Take time to plan your future. Do not let your relatives or friends, anxious for your welfare, push you into some hasty move that later you may regret. If it is financially possible for you, stay in your own home, with the familiar things about you. We need many months to become reconciled to the loss that has overtaken us; and if at first the silence of the empty house may seem unbearable, do not forget it is still the home you shared, which two persons made their own.

As the months pass and the seasons change, something of tranquillity descends, and although the well-remembered footstep will not sound again, nor the voice call from the room beyond, there seems to be about one in the air an atmosphere of love, a living presence. I say this in no haunting sense, ghosts, and phantoms are far from my mind. It is as though one shared, in some indefinable manner, the freedom and the peace, even at times the joy, of another world where there is no more pain. It is not a question of faith or of belief. It is not necessary to be a follower of any religious doctrine to become aware of what I mean. It is not the prerogative of the devout. The feeling is simply there, pervading all thought, all action. When Christ the healer said, "Blessed are they that mourn, for they shall be comforted," he must have meant just this.

Later, if you go away, if you travel, even if you decide to make your home elsewhere, the spirit of tenderness, of love, will not desert you. You will find that it has become part of you, rising from within yourself; and because of it you are no longer fearful of loneliness, of the dark, because death, the last enemy, has been overcome.

Coping

Three American poets, Lucille Clifton, Edna St. Vincent Millay and William Dickey, express, in the depression that so often characterizes the middle period of mourning, how it feels to go through the motions of living, hanging on to daily routines that seem meaningless in the face of loss.

Lucille Clifton

For deLawd

people say they have a hard time
understanding how I
go on about my business
playing my Ray Charles
hollering at the kids—
seems like my Afro
cut off in some old image
would show I got a long memory
and I come from a line
of black and going on women
who got used to making it through murdered sons
and who grief kept on pushing
who fried chicken
ironed
swept off the back steps
who grief kept
for their still alive sons
for their sons coming
for their sons gone
just pushing

Edna St. Vincent Millay
1892–1950

Lament

Listen, children:
Your father is dead.
From his old coats
I'll make you little jackets;
I'll make you little trousers
From his old pants.
There'll be in his pockets
Things he used to put there,
Keys and pennies
Covered with tobacco;
Dan shall have the pennies
To save in his bank;
Anne shall have the keys
To make a pretty noise with.
Life must go on,
And the dead be forgotten;
Life must go on,
Though good men die;
Anne, eat your breakfast;
Dan, take your medicine;
Life must go on;
I forget just why.

William Dickey

The Shortest Day

TO THE MEMORY OF RALPH DICKEY

The white room that I eat in and write in
is filled with the wet light of a winter afternoon.
It is the shortest day.

Tangerines, lemons,
bright yellow candles in bright lacquer holders.
I use these to hold on with. To try.

You yourself have taken your darkness away with you
and somewhere in this wet enormous country now
you are lying, as thin as you could ever have wished to be.

It is a little harder, here, without you.
The light lessens, and the voices of shouting children
distance themselves in the ending of this cold year.

Be at some ease. We will come walking toward you,
seeking you, to kneel clumsily, to lie down,
to move a little, until the wet earth lets us in.

Now, for you, I am lighting a candle, and another,
So as to kill myself not this night, but another.
But that is only time. When it needs to, the joining will come.

I wish I could ask you to wait for me
there where you are in the night, at least touch my hand,
at least say to me, "Quiet, now. Come in."

Afterlife and Reunion

The modern decline of belief in an afterlife doesn't lessen the strong desire of the bereaved to be in communication with the dead. Many of the writers in the next selections address the beloved as if he or she is still alive and reunion is a possibility.

Yüan Chên
779–831

An Elegy

I

O youngest, best-loved daughter of Hsieh,
Who unluckily married this penniless scholar,
You patched my clothes from your own wicker basket,
And I coaxed off your hairpins of gold, to buy wine with;
For dinner we had to pick wild herbs—
And to use dry locust-leaves for our kindling.
... Today they are paying me a hundred thousand—
And all that I can bring to you is a temple sacrifice.

II

We joked, long ago, about one of us dying,
But suddenly, before my eyes, you are gone.
Almost all your clothes have been given away;
Your needlework is sealed, I dare not look at it. ...
I continue our bounty to our men and our maids—
Sometimes, in a dream I bring you gifts.

... This is a sorrow that all mankind must know—
But not as those know it who have been poor together.

III

I sit here alone, mourning for us both.
How many years do I lack now of my threescore and ten?
There have been better men than I to whom heaven denied a son,
There was a poet better than I whose dead wife could not hear
    him.
What have I to hope for in the darkness of our tomb?
You and I had little faith in a meeting after death—
Yet my open eyes can see all night
That lifelong trouble of your brow.

Translated from the Chinese by Witter Bynner

Alice Walker

"Goodnight, Willie Lee, I'll See You in the Morning"

Looking down into my father's
dead face
for the last time
my mother said without
tears, without smiles
without regrets
but with *civility*
"Goodnight, Willie Lee, I'll see you
in the morning."
And it was then I knew that the healing
of all our wounds
is forgiveness
that permits a promise
of our return
at the end.

Else Lasker-Schüler
1876–1945

One of the greatest Jewish poets, Lasker-Schüler was associated with the German expressionist movement. After her work was banned by the Nazis, she fled to Switzerland and later to Palestine. All of her life she was preoccupied with death; her favorite brother died when she was fourteen, her mother when she was twenty-one, and the son she named for her dead brother when he was twenty-seven. This poem was written for a friend (whose real name was Johannes Holzman) who died in a Russian prison under suspicion of revolutionary activities.

To Senna Hoy

Since you lie buried in the hill
The earth is sweet.

Wherever my feet take me on tiptoe
I walk in pure ways.

O the roses of your blood
Imbue death with sweetness!

No longer am I afraid
Of death.

On your grave already I blossom
With the flowers of creepers.

Your lips have always called me,
Now my name lost its way home.

Every shovelful of earth I threw
Covered me, too.

Therefore it's always night in me
And stars already in the twilight.

And I have become incomprehensible to our friends
And truly a stranger.

But you stand at the gate of the stillest town
And wait for me, you great angel.

Translated from the German by Glauco Cambon

Ruth Stone

Being Human,

Though all the force to hold the parts together
And service love reversed, turned negative,
Fountained in self-destroying flames
And rained ash in volcanic weather;
We are still here where you left us
With our own kind: unstable strangers
Trembling in the sound waves of meaningless
Eloquence. They say we live.
They say, as they rise on the horizon
And come toward us dividing and dividing,
That we must save; that we must solve; transcend
Cohesive and repelling flesh, protoplasm, particles, and survive.
I do not doubt we will; I do not doubt all things are possible,
Even that wildest hope that we may meet beyond the grave.

Frank O'Connor
1903–1966

Requiem

Father Fogarty, the curate in Crislough, was sitting by the fire one evening when the housekeeper showed in a frail little woman of sixty or sixty-five. She had a long face, with big eyes that looked as though they had wept a great deal, and her smile lit up only the lower half of her face. Father Fogarty was a young man with a warm welcome for the suffering and the old. A man with emotions cut too big for the scale of his existence, he was forever floundering in enthusiasms and disillusionments, wranglings and reconciliations; but he had a heart like a house, and almost before the door closed behind her, he was squeezing the old woman's hand in his own two fat ones.

"You're in trouble," he said in a low voice.

"Wisha, aren't we all, Father?" she replied.

"I'm sorry, I'm sorry," he said. "Is it something I can do for you?"

"Only to say Mass for Timmy, Father."

"I'll do that, to be sure," he said comfortingly. "You're cold. Sit down a minute and warm yourself." Then he laid a big paw on her shoulder and added in a conspiratorial whisper, "Do you take anything? A drop of sherry, maybe?"

"Ah, don't be putting yourself out, Father."

"I'm not putting myself out at all. Or maybe you'd sooner a sup of whiskey. I have some damn good whiskey."

"Wisha, no, Father, I wouldn't, thanks. The whiskey goes to my head."

"It goes to my own," he replied cheerfully. "But the sherry is good, too." He didn't really know whether it was or not, because he rarely drank, but, being a hospitable man, he liked to give his visitors the best. He poured a glass of sherry for her and a small one for himself, and lit one of his favorite cheroots.

The old woman spread her transparent hands to the blaze and sipped at her wine. "Oh, isn't the heat lovely?" she exclaimed with girlish delight, showing her old gums. "And the sherry is lovely, too, Father. Now, I know you're surprised to see me, but I know all about you. They told me to come to you if I was in trouble. And there aren't many priests like that, Father. I was never one to criticize, but I have to say it."

"Ah," he said jovially, throwing himself back in his big leather chair and pulling on his cheroot, "we're like everybody else, Ma'am. A mixed lot."

"I daresay you're right," she said, "but they told me I could talk to you."

"Everyone talks to me," he said without boastfulness. It was true. There was something about him that invited more confidences than a normal man could respect, and Father Fogarty knew he was often indiscreet. "It's not your husband?" he added doubtfully.

"Ah, no, Father," she replied with a wistful smile. "Poor Jim is dead on me these fifteen years. Not, indeed, that I don't miss him just the same," she added thoughtfully. "Sometimes I find myself thinking of him, and he could be in the room with me. No, it's Timmy."

"The son?"

"No, Father. Though he was like a son to me. I never had any of my own. He was Jim's. One of the last things Jim did was to ask me to look after him, and indeed, I did my best. I did my best."

"I'm sure you did, Ma'am," said Father Fogarty, scowling behind his cheroot. He was a man who took death hard, for himself and for others. A stepchild was not the same thing, of course, but he supposed you could get just as attached to one of those. That was the trouble; you could get attached to anything if only you permitted yourself to do so, and he himself was one who had never known how to keep back. "I know how hard it is," he went on, chewing at his cheroot till his left eyebrow descended and seemed to join in the process, and he resembled nothing so much as a film gangster plotting the murder of an innocent victim. "And there's little anyone can say that will console you. All I know from my own experience is that the more loss we feel the more grateful we should be for whatever it was we had to lose. It means we had something worth grieving for. The ones I'm sorry for are the ones that go through life not even knowing what grief is. And you'd be surprised the number of them you'd meet."

"I daresay in one way they're lucky," she said broodingly, looking into the fire.

"They are not lucky, Ma'am, and don't you believe it," he said gruffly. "They miss all the things that make life worth while, without even knowing it. I had a woman in here the other night," he added, pointing his cheroot at the chair she sat in, "sitting where you're sitting now, and she told me when her husband gave the last breath she went on her knees by the bed and thanked God for taking him."

"God help us," the old woman said, clasping her hands. "I hope no one does the same thing over herself someday."

"Thanked God for taking him," Fogarty repeated with his troubled boyish frown. "What sort of mind can a woman like that have?"

"Oh, she's hard, she's hard," agreed the old woman, still looking into the fire.

"Hard as the hearthstone," he said dramatically. "My God, a man she'd lived with the best part of her life, whatever his faults might have been! Wouldn't you think at least she'd have some remorse for the things she'd done to him in all those years?"

"Oh, indeed, 'tis true," she said. "I often blamed myself over poor Jim. Sometimes I think if only I might have been a bit easier on him, he might be here yet."

"Most of us have to go through that sooner or later," he said, feeling that perhaps he had gone too far and reopened old wounds. His own old wounds were never far from breaking open, because often a light or careless word would bring back the memory of his mother and of his diabolical adolescent tempera-

ment. "We have to be careful of that, too," he added. "Because
it's not the guilty ones who go on brooding but the others—the
people who're only partly guilty, or maybe not guilty at all. That
can happen, too. I had a man here last week talking about his
wife's death, and nothing I could say would persuade him but
that he'd wronged her. And I knew for a fact that he was a husband in a million—a saint. It's something we can't afford to
indulge. It turns into a sort of cowardice before life. We have
to learn to accept our own limitations as human beings—our
selfishness and vanity and bad temper."

He spoke with passion, the passion of a man teaching a lesson he has never been able to learn himself. Something in his tone
made the old woman look at him, and her face softened into a
sweet, toothless old smile.

"Haven't you great wisdom for such a young man!" she
exclaimed admiringly.

"Great," he agreed with a jolly laugh. "I'm the biggest idiot
of them all."

But she shrugged this off. "Ah, what else were the saints?"

"Look here, Ma'am," he said, rising and standing over her
with mock gravity. "Don't you be going round talking about me
as a saint or you'll be having me sent to a punishment parish.
The poor Bishop has trouble enough on his hands without having to deal with saints. I'll say eight-o'clock Mass on Sunday for
your boy. Will that do you?"

"My boy?" she said in surprise. "But Timmy wasn't my
son, Father. Sure, I said I had no children."

"No. I took it he was your stepson."

"Is it Jim's?" she exclaimed with a laugh of genuine amuse-
ment at his mistake. "Ah, sure, Jim wasn't married before, Father.
Don't you see, that's why I had to come to you?"

"I see," he said, though he didn't and anyhow he felt it was
none of his business. The woman, after all, hadn't come to make
her confession. "What was his surname so?"

"Ah, Father," she said, still laughing but in a bewildered

way, "I'm so distracted that I can't explain myself properly. You have it all mixed up. Sure, I thought I explained it."

"You didn't explain it, Ma'am," he said, repressing his curiosity. "And anyway it's nothing to me who Timmy was. That's a matter between you and your confessor."

"My what?" she cried indignantly. "Ah, Father, you have me distracted completely now. This has nothing to do with confession. Oh, my, what's that Timmy was? If I could only think!"

"Take your time, Ma'am," he said, but he wondered what was coming next.

"A poodle!" she exclaimed. "Now I have it."

"A what?"

"A poodle—a French poodle is what they called him," she said, delighted to remember the proper term. And then her big eyes began to fill with tears. "Oh, Father, I don't know how I'm going to get on without him. He was everything to me. The house isn't the same without him."

"You don't mean you're asking me to say Mass for your *dog*?"

"Oh, I'm not asking you to do it for nothing," she added with dignity, opening her handbag.

"Are you a Catholic at all, Ma'am?" he asked sternly, fixing her with a glowering look that only seemed to amuse her. She tossed her head with a sudden saucy, girlish air.

"Wisha, what else would I be?" she asked gently, and he felt that there was nothing much he could say in reply.

"And do you know what the sacrifice of the Mass is?" he went on.

"Well, as I go every morning of my life, Father, I should have some idea," she replied, and again he had the feeling that she was laughing at him.

"And don't you know that you're asking me to commit sacrilege? Do you even know what sacrilege is?"

"Ah, what sacrilege?" she exclaimed lightly, shrugging it off. She took three five-pound notes from her old handbag. He knew she intended the money as an offering; he knew it was probably all she had in the world, and he found himself torn between blind rage and admiration.

"Here," he said. "Let me get you another drink. And put that blooming money back in your bag or you'll be losing it."

But the very sound of his voice told him that he was losing conviction. The terrible little old woman with her one idea exercised a sort of fascination over him that almost frightened him. He was afraid that if he wasn't careful he would soon find himself agreeing to do what she wanted. He poured her a drink, threw himself back again in his armchair, and at once gave way to his indignation.

"I cannot stand this damn sentimentality!" he shouted, hitting the arm of his chair with his clenched fist. "Every day of my life I have to see good Christians go without food and fire, clothes and medicine, while the rich people taunt them with the sight of their pampered pets. I tell you I can't stand it!"

"Why, then, I'm sure you're right, Father. But I'm not rich, and no poor person was ever sent away from my door with nothing, as long as I had it."

"I'm sure of that, Ma'am," he said humbly, ashamed of his outburst. "I'm sure you're a better Christian than I am, but there are different needs and different duties, and we must not confuse them. There are animal needs and human needs, and human needs and spiritual needs. Your dog has no need of the Mass."

"He was very fond of Mass. Every morning he came with me and lay down outside the chapel door."

"And *why* did you leave him outside the chapel door?" asked Fogarty.

"Why?"

"Yes, why? Wasn't it that you made a distinction between an animal and a spiritual need?"

"It was nothing of the kind," she said hotly. "It was the parish priest that asked me, because some old fools complained. Hah, but I often sneaked him in when they weren't looking, and let me tell you, Father, none of those old craw-thumpers behaved as devotionally as my Timmy. Up with the Gospel and down at the Elevation, without my saying a word to him. And don't tell me that Our Blessed Lord wasn't as pleased with Timmy as with them."

"I'm not telling you anything of the sort," he said, touched and amused. "All I am telling you is that now that your dog is dead, prayers can make no difference to him. Your dog couldn't incur guilt. Your prayers may make a difference to your husband because, like the rest of us, he did incur guilt in this life and may have to atone for it in the next."

"Ah, it's easy seen you didn't know Jim, Father. Poor Jim was innocent as a child. He never did anything wrong only taking the little sup of whiskey when I wouldn't be looking. I know he got a bit cranky when he had a drop in and I wouldn't give him any more, but sure that's a thing you wouldn't give a second thought to. . . . No, Father," she added thoughtfully, looking into the fire again, "I don't mind admitting that the first day or two after he died I wasn't easy in my mind at all. I didn't know what little thing he might have said or done on the side, unknown to me, or what little taste of punishment they might give him. I couldn't rest, thinking of him burning down there in Purgatory, with people he didn't know at all. A shy man, like that, and a man—I won't belie him—that would scream the house down if he as much as got a splinter in his nail. But then I realized that nobody in his right mind could be doing anything to him. Oh, no, Father, that's not why I get Masses said for Jim."

"Then why do you get them said for him?" Fogarty asked, though he knew the answer. His own big heart answered for him when his reason didn't.

"Sure, what other way have I of letting him know I'm thinking about him?" she asked with a childlike smile. "He's always in my mind, morning, noon, and night. And now Timmy is the same."

"And when I tell you that it makes no difference to Timmy —that Timmy can't know he's in your mind?"

"Ah, well, Father, these things are great mysteries," she replied comfortably, "and we don't know all about them yet. Oh, I
know there's a difference, and I'm not asking for anything impossible. Only one small Mass, so that he'll know. But when I
talk to people about it, you'd think I was mad from the way
they go on. They tell me he has no soul, because he never committed sin. How does anybody know he didn't commit sin? A
little child doesn't commit sin and he has a soul. No, Father," she
went on with iron determination, "I know I'm old and I have no
one to advise me, and my head isn't as good as it was, but thank
God I still have my wits about me. Believe me, Father, a dog is
no different from a child. When I was feeling low coming on to
Jim's anniversary, Timmy would know it. He'd know it as if he
could read what I was thinking, and he'd come and put his head
on my lap to show how sorry he was. And when he was sick himself, he'd get into my bed and curl up beside me, begging me
with his eyes to make him better. Yes, indeed, and when he was
dying I felt the same way about him as I felt about poor Jim—
just the way you described it, thinking of all the times I was hard
on him when he didn't deserve it at all. That is the hardest part of
it, Father, when you have to try and forgive yourself."

"I'm sure you have very little to forgive yourself for,
Ma'am," Fogarty said with a smile. "And God knows, if it was
anything I could do for you I'd do it, but this is something that,
as a priest, I can't do."

"And there's no one else I could go to? You don't think
if I went to the Bishop myself he'd let you do it?"

"I'm quite certain he wouldn't, Ma'am."

"Ah," she said bitterly as she raised herself heavily from her
chair, "if I was younger and smarter with my pen I'd write to the
Pope about it myself." She turned to the door, and Fogarty sprang
to open it for her, but the courtesy was lost on her. She looked
at him with deep mournful eyes that seemed to contain all the
loneliness in the world. "And it's wrong, Father, wrong," she
said in a firm voice. "I'm as good a Catholic as the next, but I'd
say it to the Pope himself this minute if he walked into this room.

They *have* souls, and people are only deluding themselves about it. Anything that can love has a soul. Show me that bad woman that thanked God her husband was dead and I'll show you some-one that maybe hasn't a soul, but don't tell me that my Timmy hadn't one. And I know as I'm standing here that somewhere or other I'll see him again."

"I hope you do, Ma'am," he said, his big voice suddenly growing gentle and timorous. "And whenever you say a prayer for him, don't forget to add one for me."

"I will not indeed, Father," she said quietly. "I know you're a good man, and I'll remember you with the others that were good to me, and one of these days, with God's help, we'll all be together again."

Alfred, Lord Tennyson
1809–1892

from Maud

O that t'were possible
After long grief and pain
To find the arms of my true love
Round me once again! . . .

A shadow flits before me,
Not thou, but like to thee:
Ah Christ! that it were possible
For one short hour to see
The souls we loved, that they might tell us
What and where they be.

John Webster
1580–1625

from *The Duchess of Malfi*

O that it were possible we might
But hold some two dayes conference with the dead!
From them I should learne somewhat, I am sure
I never shall know here.

Ambivalence, Relief, Regrets

The next selections show the various ways the dead have an afterlife in the form of a continuing influence on their survivors. This seems to be particularly true when they leave us with un-resolved feelings of anger or guilt. The living may feel relief when death ends parental demands on our energies or a long and painful illness. If part of the process of bereavement is a search for the beloved, we also allow the dead to seek us out, until gradually we come to terms with their claims and ask them to let us be.

Adrienne Rich

A Woman Mourned by Daughters

Now, not a tear begun,
we sit here in your kitchen,
spent, you see, already.
You are swollen till you strain
this house and the whole sky.
You, whom we so often
succeeded in ignoring!
You are puffed up in death
like a corpse pulled from the sea;
we groan beneath your weight.
And yet you were a leaf,
a straw blown on the bed,
you had long since become
crisp as a dead insect.
What is it, if not you,

that settles on us now
like satin you pulled down
over our bridal heads?
What rises in our throat
like food you prodded in?
Nothing could be enough.
You breathe upon us now
through solid assertions
of yourself: teaspoons, goblets,
seas of carpet, a forest
of old plants to be watered,
an old man in an adjoining
room to be touched and fed.
And all this universe
dares us to lay a finger
anywhere, save exactly
as you would wish it done.

Anonymous

Traditional Women's Song of Algeria

Be happy for me, girls,
my mother-in-law is dead!
In the morning I found her
stiff, her mouth shut.
Yet I won't believe it
till I see the grass
waving on her tomb.

Recorded by Mostefa Lacheraf
Translated by Willis Barnstone

Charlotte Brontë
1816–1855

On the Death of Anne Brontë

There's little joy in life for me,
   And little terror in the grave;
I've lived the parting hour to see
   Of one I would have died to save.

Calmly to watch the failing breath,
   Wishing each sigh might be the last;
Longing to see the shade of death
   O'er those beloved features cast;

The cloud, the stillness that must part
   The darling of my life from me;
And then to thank God from my heart,
   To thank him well and fervently;

Although I knew that we had lost
   The hope and glory of our life;
And now, benighted, tempest-tossed,
   Must bear alone the weary strife.

Virginia Woolf
1882–1941

from *The Diary of Virginia Woolf, Volume 3*
WEDNESDAY 28 NOVEMBER

1928

Father's birthday. He would have been $\frac{1832}{96}$ 96, yes, today; &

could have been 96, like other people one has known; but mercifully was not. His life would have entirely ended mine. What
would have happened? No writing, no books;—inconceivable. I
used to think of him & mother daily; but writing The Light-
house, laid them in my mind. And now he comes back sometimes,
but differently. (I believe this to be true—that I was obsessed by
them both, unhealthily; & writing of them was a necessary act.)
He comes back now more as a contemporary. I must read him
some day. I wonder if I can feel again, I hear his voice, I know
this by heart?

Sandra Gilbert

After a Death

FOR MY FATHER

I am far away from you.
In my front yard the uncontrollable rain
coats leaves and bark
with a medicinal, protective sheen.

What I inherit is impossible:
a car I can't drive,

empty coats in a closet,
a useless middle initial.

I am astonished by my calm.
Have you really left me no pain?
The enormous sky, floodlit by thunder,
recalls your cold home—

the comforting grass,
the black socket of stone
in which you are fixed
like a blind eye, directionless.

William Wordsworth
1770–1850

She Dwelt Among the Untrodden Ways

She dwelt among the untrodden ways
   Beside the springs of Dove,
A maid whom there were none to praise
   And very few to love.

A violet by a mossy stone
   Half-hidden from the eye!
Fair as a star, when only one
   Is shining in the sky.

She lived unknown, and few could know
   When Lucy ceased to be;
But she is in her grave, and, oh,
   The difference to me!

Anne Sexton
1928–1974

The Truth the Dead Know

FOR MY MOTHER, BORN MARCH 1902, DIED MARCH 1959
AND MY FATHER, BORN FEBRUARY 1900, DIED JUNE 1959

Gone, I say and walk from church,
refusing the stiff procession to the grave,
letting the dead ride alone in the hearse.
It is June. I am tired of being brave.

We drive to the Cape. I cultivate
myself where the sun gutters from the sky,
where the sea swings in like an iron gate
and we touch. In another country people die.

My darling, the wind falls in like stones
from the whitehearted water and when we touch
we enter touch entirely. No one's alone.
Men kill for this, or for as much.

And what of the dead? They lie without shoes
in their stone boats. They are more like stone
than the sea would be if it stopped. They refuse
to be blessed, throat, eye and knucklebone.

Maxine Kumin

Poet and novelist Maxine Kumin was a close friend of Anne Sexton. The two were together earlier on the day in 1974 when Anne Sexton took her own life.

How It Is

Shall I say how it is in your clothes?
A month after your death I wear your blue jacket.
The dog at the center of my life recognizes
you've come to visit, he's ecstatic.
In the left pocket, a hole.
In the right, a parking ticket
delivered up last August on Bay State Road.
In my heart, a scatter like milkweed,
a flinging from the pods of the soul.
My skin presses your old outline.
It is hot and dry inside.

I think of the last day of your life,
old friend, how I would unwind it, paste
it together in a different collage,
back from the death car idling in the garage,
back up the stairs, your praying hands unlaced,
reassembling the bites of bread and tuna fish
into a ceremony of sandwich,
running the home movie backward to a space
we could be easy in, a kitchen place
with vodka and ice, our words like living meat.

Dear friend, you have excited crowds
with your example. They swell
like wine bags, straining at your seams.
I will be years gathering up our words,

fishing out letters, snapshots, stains,
leaning my ribs against this durable cloth
to put on the dumb blue blazer of your death.

Ann Stanford

The Fathers

I am beset by spirits, layer on layer
They hover over our sleep in the quilted air.
The owl calls and the spirits hang and listen.
Over our breaths, over our hearts they press.
They are wings and eyes, and they come surely to bless
There is hardly room for the crowd of them under the ceiling.

Remember me, remember me, they whisper.

The dark rustles, their faces all are dim.
They know me well, I represent them here.
I keep their lands, their gold and fruiting orchards,
I keep their books, their rings, their testaments.

I am their blood of life made visible
I hold their part of life that vanishes.
They whisper to me, names and messages,
Lost in the world, a sifting down of shadows.

I am myself, I say, it is my blood
It is my time of sun and lifting of green,
Nothing is here, but what I touch and see.
They cry out *we are here in the root and tree.*
It is my night, I say—and yours for sleeping.
They move their wings, I think I hear them weeping.
Blest spirits, let me be.

Josephine Miles

Sorrow

A tall stature of
Grave sorrow
Is what I embrace, its tenderness
Doesn't bend to me.
Straight

Sorrow descended
From cries in trees
Stands upright
Stiff at its waist
Where I reach,

Tells me but does not
Tell me.
Rather witholds
More than I can
More than man can.

Marcel Proust
1871–1922

from *Letters*

FROM A LETTER TO THE COMTESSE DE NOAILLES, 1903

You, who saw Father only two or three times, have no way of
knowing how kind and simple he was. I tried—if not exactly to
satisfy him, for I am well aware that I was always the disappointment of his life—at least to show him my affection. At the same

time, there were days when I revolted against some of his remarks which seemed to me too sure, too positive, and the other
Sunday, I remember, in a political discussion I said some things I
shouldn't have. I can't tell you how unhappy I am about it now.
It seems as though I had been harsh with someone who even
then was no longer able to defend himself. I'd give anything if
only I had been all affection and gentleness that evening. But I
almost always was. Father's nature was so much nobler than
mine. I am always complaining. Father's only thought when he
was ill was to keep us from knowing about it. However, these
are things I can't yet bear to think about. They cause me so much
grief. Life has started again. If only I had an aim, an ambition
of any kind, it would help me to bear it. But that isn't the case.
My own vague happiness was only the reflection of Father's and
Mother's, which I always saw around me, not without remorse,
which is even sharper now because I was only its shadow. Now
the little incidents in life which made up my happiness are filled
with pain. However, it is life starting again, and not just a blunt
and brief despair, which could only be temporary. So I shall soon
be able to see you again, and I promise no longer selfishly to talk
to you about things I can't even explain, because I never spoke
of them. I can almost say that I never thought of them. They
were my life. But I didn't realize it.

Witter Bynner
1881–1968

Pause

We cannot stay their death nor stay our death.
We can but pause and look into a glass
And see our nostrils taking in the breath
Which is the breath of life it always was.
We can touch our flesh and with a certain pride

Feel it still warm, can remember tender things
We used to say to someone who has died,
Can still be glad of present happenings,
Can still be glad that they, not we have gone
Into that shadow of eternity
Which we are not compelled to look upon
As long as there are lesser things to see.
What else is there to do, although a face
Lies quietly in its eventual place.

James Joyce
1882–1941

The Irish poet and novelist James Joyce lost his father at the
time his only grandson was born.

Ecce Puer

Of the dark past
A child is born
With joy and grief
My heart is torn.

Calm in his cradle
The living lies.
May love and mercy
Unclose his eyes!

Young life is breathed
On the glass;
The world that was not
Comes to pass.

A child is sleeping:
An old man gone.
O, father forsaken,
Forgive your son!

Galway Kinnell

The Last Hiding Places of Snow

I
The burnt tongue
fluttered, "I'm dying . . ."
and then, "Why did . . . ? Why . . . ?"
What earthly knowledge did she still need
just then, when
the tongue failed
or began speaking in another direction?

Only the struggle for breath
remained: groans made
of all the goodbyes ever spoken all
turned meaningless; surplus world sucked back
into a body laboring to live
all the way to death; and past death, if it must.

There is a place in the woods
where you can hear
such sounds: sighs, groans
seeming to come
from the darkness of spruce boughs,
from glimmer-at-night of the white birches,
from the last hiding places of snow,

a breeze,
that's all, driving
across certain obstructions: every stump
speaks,
the spruce needles play out of the air
the sorrows cried into it somewhere else.

Once in a while, passing the place,
I have imagined I heard
my old mother calling, thinking out loud her
mother-love toward me, over those many miles
from where her bones lie,
five years
in earth now, with my father's thirty-years' bones.

I have always felt
anointed by her love, its light
like sunlight
falling through broken panes
onto the floor
of a deserted house: we may go, it remains,
telling of goodness of being, of permanence.

So lighted I have believed
I could wander anywhere,
among any foulnesses, any contagions,
I could climb through the entire empty world
and find my way back and learn again to be happy.

But when I've stopped and listened,
all I've heard was
what may once have been speech
or groans, now
shredded to a hiss from passing
through the whole valley of spruce needles.

My mother did not want me to be born;
afterwards, all her life, she needed me to return.
When this more-than-love flowed toward me, it brought
    darkness;
she wanted me as burial earth wants—to heap itself gently upon
    but also to annihilate—
and I knew, whenever I felt longings to go back,
that is what wanting to die is. That is why

dread lives in me,
dread which comes when what gives life beckons toward death,
dread which throws through me
waves
of utter strangeness, which wash the entire world empty.

II
I was not at her bedside
that final day, I did not grant her ancient,
huge-knuckled hand
its last wish, I did not let it
gradually become empty of the son's hand—and so
hand her, with more steadiness, into the future.
Instead, old age took her
by force, though with the help
of her old, broken attachments
which had broken
only on this side of death
but had kept intact on the other.

I would know myself lucky if my own children
could be at my deathbed, to take
my hand in theirs and with theirs
to bless me back into the world as I leave,
with smoothness pressed into roughness,
with folding-light fresh runner hands to runner of wasted breath,
with mortal touch whose mercy two bundled-up figures greeting

on a freezing morning, exposing the ribboned ends of right
arms, entwining these, squeeze back and forth before
walking on,
with memories these hands keep, of strolling down Bethune
Street in spring, a little creature hanging from each arm, by
a hand so small it can do no more than press its tiny thumb
pathetically into the soft beneath my thumb . . .

But for my own mother I was not there . . .
and at the gates of the world, therefore, between
holy ground
and ground of almost all its holiness gone, I loiter
in stupid fantasies I can live that day again.

Why did you come so late?
Why will you go too early?

I know now there are regrets
we can never be rid of;
permanent remorse. Knowing this, I know also
I am to draw from that surplus stored up
of tenderness which was hers by right,
and which no one ever gave her,
and give it away, freely.

III
A child, a little girl,

in violet hat, blue scarf, green sweater, yellow skirt, orange
socks, red boots,
on a rope swing, swings
in sunlight
over a garden in Ireland, backfalls,
backrises,
forthsinks,
forthsoars, her charmed life holding its breath

innocent of groans, beyond any
future, far past the past: into a pure present.

Now she wears rhythmically into the air
of morning
the rainbow's curve, but upside down
so that angels may see
beloved dross promising heaven:
no matter what fire we invent to destroy us,
ours will have been the brightest world ever existing . . .
The vision breaks,
the child suddenly grows old, she dies . . .

Every so often, when I look
at the dark sky, I know she remains
among the old endless blue lightedness
of stars; or finding myself out in a field
in November, when a strange
starry perhaps first snowfall blows
down across the darkening air, lightly,
I know she is there, where snow
falls flakes down fragile softly
falling until I can't see the world
any longer, only its stilled shapes.

Even now when I wake at night
in some room far from everyone,
the darkness sometimes
lightens a little, and then,
because of nothing,
in spite of nothing,
in an imaginary daybreak, I see her
and for that moment I am still her son
and I am in the holy land
and twice in the holy land, remembered
within her, and remembered in the memory
her old body slowly executes into the earth.

Summer and Fall

Then let not winter's ragged hand deface
In thee thy summer, ere thou be distilled.
                    —William Shakespeare, Sonnet VI

Memory

One of the earliest definitions of memory is "a service for the dead." For some writers in the next selections, memory becomes a means of preserving the presence of the dead so that, finally, there is no sense of loss. For others, the gradual dimming of memory, although often observed ruefully, is acknowledged as a necessary relinquishment of the past. This passing of sorrow brings its own silence, quite different from the hush of early grief.

Emily Dickinson
1830–1886

341

After great pain, a formal feeling comes—
The Nerves sit ceremonious, like Tombs—
The stiff Heart questions was it He, that bore,
And Yesterday, or Centuries before?

The Feet, mechanical, go round—
Of Ground, or Air, or Ought—
A Wooden way
Regardless grown,
A Quartz contentment, like a stone—

This is the Hour of Lead—
Remembered, if outlived,
As Freezing persons, recollect the Snow—
First—Chill—then Stupor—then the letting go—

Alfred, Lord Tennyson
1809–1892

from *In Memoriam A.H.H.*

Peace; come away: the song of woe
   Is after all an earthly song.
   Peace; come away: we do him wrong
To sing so wildly: let us go.

Thomas Moore
1779–1852

"Oft in the Stilly Night" is the song that comes unbidden to comfort Mrs. Bagot in Maeve Brennan's story "The Eldest Child," reprinted in the first part of this collection.

Oft in the Stilly Night

Oft, in the stilly night,
   Ere Slumber's chain has bound me,
Fond Memory brings the light
   Of other days around me:
      The smiles, the tears,
      Of boyhood's years,
   The words of love then spoken;
      The eyes that shone,
      Now dimmed and gone,
   The cheerful hearts now broken!
Thus in the stilly night,
   Ere Slumber's chain has bound me,

Sad Memory brings the light
   Of other days around me.

When I remember all
   The friends so linked together
I've seen around me fall,
   Like leaves in wintry weather,
     I feel like one
     Who treads alone
   Some banquet-hall deserted,
     Whose lights are fled,
     Whose garlands dead,
   And all but him departed!
Thus in the stilly night,
   Ere Slumber's chain has bound me,
Sad Memory brings the light
   Of other days around me.

Colette
1873–1954

from *My Mother's House*

It is the image in the mind that links us to our lost treasures; but
it is the loss that shapes the image, gathers the flowers, weaves
the garland.

Marcel Proust
1871–1922

from *Letters*

. . . memory nourishes the heart, and grief abates.

Barbara Howes

A Letter from the Caribbean

Breezeways in the tropics winnow the air,
Are ajar to its least breath
But hold back, in a feint of architecture,
The boisterous sun
Pouring down upon

The island like a cloudburst. They
Slant to loft air, they curve, they screen
The wind's wild gaiety
Which tosses palm
Branches about like a marshal's plumes.

Within this filtered, latticed
World, where spools of shadow
Form, lift and change,
The triumph of incoming air
Is that it is there,

Cooling and salving us. Louvers,
Trellises, vines—music also—
Shape the arboreal wind, make skeins
Of it, and a maze
To catch shade. The days

Are all variety, blowing;
Aswirl in a perpetual current
Of wind, shadow, sun,
I marvel at the capacity
Of memory

Which, in some deep pocket
Of my mind, preserves you whole—

As wind is wind, as the lion-taming
Sun is sun, you are, you stay:
Nothing is lost, nothing has blown away.

D. H. Lawrence
1885–1930

Brooding Grief

A yellow leaf, from the darkness
Hops like a frog before me;
Why should I start and stand still?

I was watching the woman that bore me
Stretched in the brindled darkness
Of the sick-room, rigid with will
To die: and the quick leaf tore me
Back to this rainy swill
Of leaves and lamps and the city street mingled
          before me.

Willis Barnstone

Disappearance
FOR MY MOTHER

When they lowered you in the earth
We wept under the summer sun.
The rocking of the coffin stopped
and our small party went away.
You left so quickly from the light
almost no one of the great earth

observed the moment of your death.
We few who know your quiet life
try to remember, but forget,
and neither memory nor love
will bring you daylight in the grave.
Your life was brief—a morning walk.
We whom you loved still know at times
a quiet absence in the noon.

Peter Everwine

Counting

A wall collapses

An arm starts flopping
like a headless chicken

Next day
combing the rubble
they add the 1 and the 2
The 3

The living gather the numbers
and go on with their living
counting the days and the months

Counting the insults the spoons the stars
the stacks of dimes the drawers

It is the dead
who keep diminishing

My father whose face I barely recall
lost some fingers
in a machine

Sometimes I count them
when I can't sleep
The 2 and the 3

The 1 is always me
sewing an endless seam

Gërard de Nerval
1808–1855

The Grandmother

Here it is three years since my grandmother died
—That old woman—there at her funeral,
Parents and friends, everyone was in tears,
From sadness that was bitter as it was real.

Alone I wandered through the house, bewildered
Rather than shocked; after, when I drew near
To her coffin someone did complain of me
Finding me neither beside myself nor in tears.

Noisy sorrows are quickly over and done:
Many other emotions, three years later,
Complete change—whether for good or ill—
Have washed the memory of her from their hearts.

I, I only, dream on and weep for her
Often; three years later, taking strength

From the passage of time, like letters cut on bark
Her memory, too, deepens as time lengthens.

                      Translated from the French by Barbara Howes

Emily Brontë
1818–1848

Remembrance

Cold in the earth—and the deep snow piled above thee,
    Far, far removed, cold in the dreary grave!
Have I forgot, my only Love, to love thee,
    Severed at last by Time's all-severing wave?

Now, when alone, do my thoughts no longer hover
    Over the mountains, on that northern shore,
Resting their winds where heath and fern-leaves cover
    Thy noble heart for ever, ever more?

Cold in the earth—and fifteen wild Decembers
    From those brown hills, have melted into spring:
Faithful, indeed, is the spirit that remembers
    After such years of change and suffering!

Sweet Love of youth, forgive, if I forget thee,
    While the world's tide is bearing me along;
Other desires and others hopes beset me,
    Hopes which obscure, but cannot do thee wrong!

No later light has lightened up my heaven,
    No second morn has ever shone for me;
All my life's bliss from thy dear life was given,
    All my life's bliss is in the grave with thee.

But when the days of golden dreams had perish'd,
   And even Despair was powerless to destroy,
Then did I learn how existence could be cherished,
   Strengthened, and fed, without the aid of joy.

Then did I check the tears of useless passion—
   Weaned my young soul from yearning after thine,
Sternly denied its burning wish to hasten
   Down to that tomb already more than mine.

And, even yet, I dare not let it languish,
   Dare not indulge in memory's rapturous pain;
Once drinking deep of that divinest anguish,
   How could I seek the empty world again?

William Wordsworth
1770–1850

Sonnet on Catherine Wordsworth

Surprised by joy—impatient as the Wind
I turned to share the transport—O! with whom
But Thee, deep buried in the silent tomb,
That spot which no vicissitude can find?
Love, faithful love, recalled thee to my mind—
But how could I forget thee? Through what power,
Even for the least division of an hour,
Have I been so beguiled as to be blind
To my most grievous loss? That thought's return
Was the worst pang that sorrow ever bore,
Save one, one only, when I stood forlorn,
Knowing my heart's best treasure was no more;
That neither present time, nor years unborn
could to my sight that heavenly face restore.

Marcel Proust
1871–1922

from *Letters*

. . . you will be not cured, but . . . one day—an idea that will
horrify you now—this intolerable misfortune will become a
blessed memory of a being who will never again leave you. But
you are in a stage of unhappiness where it is impossible for you
to have faith in these reassurances.

Louise Bogan
1897–1970

Zone

We have struck the regions wherein we are keel or reef.
The wind breaks over us,
And against high sharp angles almost splits into words,
And these are of fear or grief.

Like a ship, we have struck expected latitudes
Of the universe, in March.
Through one short segment's arch
Of the zodiac's round
We pass,
Thinking: Now we hear
What we heard last year,
And bear the wind's rude touch
And its ugly sound
Equally with so much
We have learned how to bear.

Dreaming the Dead

Even when the dead have ebbed in memory from our waking hours, they may return to us in dreams. These reunions, often startlingly vivid in their imagery, are sometimes comforting. Or, on wakening, they may leave us feeling bereft, as if our unconscious is reminding us that we have not yet fully accepted the cruelty of the loss or have feelings still to be resolved.

A Japanese Court Lady
?–671

On the Death of Emperor Tenji

I am of this world,
Unfit to touch a god.
Separated from his spirit,
In the morning I grieve my Lord:
Sundered from his soul,
I long for my Lord.
Would he were jade
I might coil on my arm!
Would he were a robe
I might never put off!
I saw my Lord,
The one I love,
Last night . . . in sleep.

Translated from the Japanese
by Geoffrey Bownas and Anthony Thwaite

John Milton
1608–1674

Katherine Woodcock, Milton's second wife, died at the age of thirty, four months after the birth of a child.

Methought I Saw My Late Espousèd Saint

Methought I saw my late espousèd saint
    Brought to me like Alcestis from the grave,
    Whom Jove's great son to her glad husband gave,
    Rescued from death by force, though pale and
        faint.
Mine, as whom washed from spot of child-bed
        taint
    Purification in the Old Law did save,
    And such as yet once more I trust to have
    Full sight of her in Heaven without restraint,
Came vested all in white, pure as her mind.
    Her face was veiled, yet to my fancied sight
    Love, sweetness, goodness, in her person
        shined
So clear as in no face with more delight.
    But O as to embrace me she inclined,
    I waked, she fled, and day brought back my
        night.

Phil George

A Nez-Percé-Tsimshian, Phil George's Indian name is Two
Swans Ascending from Still Waters.

The Visit

Grandmother, I dreamed of you again—
I burned the sage you
    sent when I was in Vietnam.
Before you died—
    and I could not come home.
Beside my bed is the Spruce Bough
    to keep nightmares away.

Today I will visit you beside
    Our Stream—at Arrow.
I will sprinkle tobacco on waters:
    They will thank me.

Grandmother, let's visit—
    Talk and laugh when
    Sun is shining;
So I may sleep, rest at night.

Edmund Wilson
1895–1972

In 1932, two years after their marriage, Wilson's second wife,
Margaret Canby, died in an accidental fall. Wilson had kept
private journals since youth, and in the volume titled *The Thirties*, edited by Leon Edel and published after Wilson's death, he

speaks of dreams about his wife that were to recur for many years. In his introduction, Leon Edel says, "The dreams suggest profound and unresolved feelings, continuing grief and self-blame; he had a strange sense that in dying she had abandoned him; and then the opposite, he felt guilty, as if he had abandoned her."

His dream search for her is one of frustration; something always happens to keep them separated. Elsewhere in the journals he remarks, "After she was dead I loved her," intimating that perhaps the reason he cannot find her again is that he is not looking for the Margaret of their married life but for a version free of human foibles.

---

from *The Thirties*

NEW YORK, 53rd STREET, 1932–33

Margaret. —Her death which deprived her of the things we have in life made them seem worthless to me—I couldn't enjoy them so much because they were things which could be spoiled for her and taken away from her. A loyalty to her had made me less loyal to life itself. I felt toward life in general some of the resentment I had toward the undertaker, etc. (at the same time slight quiet symptoms of sadistic satisfaction). Such things, satisfactions—books, love-making, drinking, talking, enjoyment of sensations—were not serious since they could be cut off from someone as fine and serious as she—as the part of me that had died with her. Scorn of life itself—when someone you love dies, you feel that it does not make much difference having it come to an end. Why should you accept something which has been taken away from someone who deserved it as much—your true comradeship with her, true solidarity with what she represents for you that is noble, is to challenge life, to be proud to take it seriously, to go on paying no attention its attractions, diversions, demands, toward things of higher importance (life in the sense of such little flashby of individual sensations as the individual can experience).

—Her books, *Fear, Psychoanalyzing Ourselves*—where I had a partial outlet in radical writing, etc.—she had had none except sex, which I had shut down on last winter. . . .

Dream. There she was alive—what was the catch?—that she was supposed not to exist any more—but there she was, and what was to prevent our living together again?—*that* would be just a gap in the past. —The present of her being alive and of our being together again was real—the future could be real, too.

I dreamed again May 13 [1933] that it was merely a question of her being sick and that when she got well, we'd be together—I stupidly hadn't realized that, had thought it would separate us for good so that I wouldn't see her any more—and couldn't help thinking the next Monday, What if she should come in the door?

The two rock hinds in the aquarium, one lying up against the other and on top of her against the rock side of the tank, gave me a sensation faintly gratifying—why? —and then I realized it was because that was the way we used to be in bed together, faced in the same direction and I with my arms around her—one on top shifted up, then back into place, fixed himself better.

Dream. Thought in dim grayish dream I could tell her how silly I'd been about making mistake about not being able to see her again.

Morning of Eliot hangover, I missed her little round body—we used to recover from hangovers together—I used to turn myself around and lie with my face against her feet.

Dream. I went back to her father's room, with the bureau I have no or one like it, in the old house at Red Bank—she was angry with me: While you were doing (something), I've been here all alone!—she was getting dressed.

—But in a sense I could have nothing in common with her any more—she was dead and I was still living. . . .

Dream. She was ill and supposed not to have long to live, lying on a bed somewhere we had gone to see a woman doctor— as we were talking, it occurred to me that she might get well, and if I could make her believe that I loved her and wanted her to get well, the trouble might disappear—I told her that she must get well, that she wasn't so seriously sick—she said she didn't know whether she was going to like what the doctor would tell her to do—I told her about my dreams, how I had thought we were back at the Berkeley, etc., and then waked up to find she was dead, but now she didn't need to die, there was time for me to convince her I wanted her to get well—yet I asked myself, were the other possibilities of getting some other more con-genial, more intellectually developed woman able to tempt me? now that I could have her again, was the same doubt and negative feeling toward her that had kept us apart cropping up again? did I find now that I thought I could have her again that I wanted her less than I had in the dream in the Berkeley when I couldn't have her because she was dead? —I decided I did want her, yes, and I could have her, and persuade her to live. —Woke up among all the green foliage and lovely peace of a slightly over-cast June Sunday at Red Bank. . . .

STAMFORD, 1936

Dreams about Margaret—I have begun having these dreams about Margaret again out here in the Stamford house—it is as if I kept trying to make the thing more probable, put up more obstacles to surmount between myself and the reality. . . .

In this dream I had tried to safeguard myself: I didn't see

her as I had before—there were obstacles, an attempt to do away with the impossibility of reality, but they were obstacles which could be overcome: I kept telling myself that I had never seen her dead, that it was obviously not true that she was dead, as people told me of her being around—and even after I woke up I had to recall to myself that I had certainly seen her dead in the funeral parlor at Santa Barbara—that I had seen her pale and smooth and hard and rigid in death and now could never see her talking and affectionate, a little live human girl, again in New York, as I had thought I was going to in the dream. —Shy and warm, inarticulate and lively. . . .

Dream about Margaret, early December 1936—at Stamford. My subconscious mind had invented a new device: I thought there was another woman who resembled her exactly and who was still alive. She resembled Margaret so closely that we even had memories in common of our earlier life together. I saw her, and we arranged to marry, but then she was dining with somebody else that night, and I let her go without getting her telephone number or her address. Then I realized that if I could find out, I could be with her that night—could love her and sleep with her. I saw her in my mind in her slip. As I was trying to think of someone who knew where she was, I woke up. . . .

1937

Dream about Margaret. This time I thought I had found somebody different who looked exactly like her—so that I couldn't be deceived again by finding out I couldn't have her. . . .

1939–1940

Margaret. For years, I have been like a spring, uncoiled with difficulty and kept straight with effort, that snaps back into its twisted state as soon as sleep begins to relax the effort: the images that disguise reversion to the past, the convulsive twitching that wakes me up and represents the reassertion of the effort that keeps me straight by day.

Mary Jane Moffat

The night of my husband's death as I packed clothes to take to
the funeral home, impulsively I placed in a pocket a snapshot
of our last island vacation together, a time of particular happiness.
This image was returned to me several months later in a dream.

In This New Year

I saw you on the street last night
and left my lovers and walked
easily into your familiar arms.
You smelled not of grave-rags
but like home: coffee and the rain-soaked
newspaper curling in the oven.

You spoke to me in captions of all
that death has to offer—a resort
where tropic waters bear you weightless
in a long and perfect drunk, and desire
is just a word, like *palmtree* or *fish*.

You showed me the snapshot of that
lurid sunset I put in your pocket
when I packed your tourist clothes.
Salt had bled the colors,
no more horizon.

You leaned to kiss me
in the place only you know
and I turned away
and left you for the river
smell of living men.

Olga Berggolts

A native of Leningrad, during Stalin's purges of the thirties Berggolts was imprisoned, her husband executed. Her second husband died of hunger during the German blockade of Leningrad in 1942. She is best known for her *Leningrad Notebook*. The title she gives this poem suggests the persistence of loyalty in the unconscious, even when the survivor has entered a new relationship.

Infidelity

Not waking, in my dreams, my dreams,
I saw you—you were alive.
You had endured all and come to me,
crossing the last frontier.

You were earth already, ashes, you
were my glory, my punishment.
But, in spite of life,
                of death,
you rose from your thousand
                                graves.

You passed through war hell, concentration camp,
through furnace, drunk with the flames,
through your own death you entered Leningrad,
came out of love for me.

You found my house, but I live now
not in our house, in another;
and a new husband shares my waking hours ...
O how could you not have known?

Like the master of the house, proudly you crossed
the threshold, stood there lovingly.
And I murmured: "God will rise again,"
and made the sign of the cross
over you—the unbeliever's cross, the cross
of despair, as black as pitch,
the cross that was made over each house
that winter, that winter in which

you died.

    O my friend, forgive me
as I sigh. How long have I not known
where waking ends and the dream begins . . .

              Translated from the Russian by Daniel Weissbort

Carl Bode

Requiem

So. They and I are back from the outside,
Sitting in the cold sunlight of the parlour.
We agree, with no pride,
That we never saw so many lovely flowers.
Petals still lie on the rug; the heavy scent has not died.

There is not much else for us to talk
About really—not much to say or do,
Except to get up and walk
Around in the cold, scented sunlight; so I sit
Looking down, and pull into strands a piece of flower stalk.

I think, of course, of that night last year
When I dreamt that you need not have died, so that my
Mind was filled with a dull, queer
Kind of loneliness which would not go away for
A long while; I remember it well as I sit here.

And I well remember those flowers,
Thick leaves with dust on them, coarse hairy stems
Forced by late summer showers.
The blooms were large and had a flat, metallic
Odour. They were bouquets of love, they were ours.

Presences and Apparitions

An eerie phenomenon that defies rational analysis and cuts across religious belief is the sense that the dead person is among us. The sensation can take many forms, from a heightened awareness of the spiritual presence of the dead to fully dressed apparitions.

An unexpected or violent death, in particular, may require a good-bye that can be satisfied only by a reinvention of the dead person's essence, as in the selection from *A Death in the Family* in the next group of writings. If such a farewell is not accomplished, a survivor may feel haunted, like Emily Brontë's fictional Heathcliff, who literally must dig up his Cathy in order to put both their spirits to rest. Pearl Buck's eventual relinquishment of her husband's presence clearly is a saner form of concluding the search, but to demonstrate how differently our psyches heal, R. K. Narayan's English teacher's tender reunion with his wife is a radiant fictive version of incorporation of the dead person's spirit within the being of the mourner. In these writings we see that in one form or another, the search does end, from William Maxwell's realization that he no longer needs his mother to Linda Hartman's necessity to personify death itself before she defuses its power over her life.

James Agee
1909–1955

In the scene that precedes this excerpt, Mary Follet and her family are gathered in the Follet living room trying to absorb the news that Mary's husband, Jay, has just been killed in an automobile accident. One by one several in the group become

aware of a presence other than themselves in the house. A conflict in the marriage had been Mary's devout religious faith, and
when she senses that the spirit has moved to her children's room,
she follows it.

---

from *A Death in the Family*

When she came through the door of the children's room she
could feel his presence as strongly throughout the room as if
she had opened a furnace door; the presence of his strength, of
virility, of helplessness, and of pure calm. She fell down on her
knees in the middle of the floor and whispered, "Jay. My dear.
My dear one. You're all right now, darling. You're not troubled
any more, are you, my darling? Not any more. Not ever any
more, dearest. I can feel how it is with you. I know, my dearest.
It's terrible to go. You don't want to. Of *course* you don't. But
you've got to. And you know they're going to be all right. Everything is going to be all right, my darling. God take you. God
keep you, my own beloved. God make His light to shine upon
you." And even while she whispered, his presence became faint,
and in a moment of terrible dread she cried out "Jay!" and hurried to her daughter's crib. "Stay with me just one minute," she
whispered, "just one minute, my dearest"; and in some force he
did return; she felt him with her, watching his child. Catherine
was sleeping with all her might and her thumb was deep in her
mouth; she was scowling fiercely. "Mercy, child," Mary whispered,
smiling, and touched her hot forehead to smooth it, and she
growled. "God bless you, God keep you," her mother whispered,
and came silently to her son's bed. There was the cap in its tissue
paper, beside him on the floor; he slept less deeply than his
sister, with his chin lifted, and his forehead flung back; he looked
grave, serene and expectant.

"Be with us all you can," she whispered. "This is good-bye."
And again she went to her knees. Good-bye, she said again,
within herself; but she was unable to feel much of anything.

"God help me to *realize* it," she whispered, and clasped her hands before her face: but she could realize only that he was fading, and that it was indeed good-bye, and that she was at that moment unable to be particularly sensitive to the fact.

And now he was gone entirely from the room, from the house and from this world.

"Soon, Jay. Soon, dear," she whispered; but she knew that it would not be soon. She knew that a long life lay ahead of her, for the children were to be brought up, and God alone could know what change and chance might work upon them all, before they met once more. She felt at once calm and annihilating emptiness, and a cold and overwhelming fullness.

"God help us all," she whispered. "May God in His loving mercy keep us all."

She signed herself with the Cross and left the room.

She looks as she does when she has just received, Hannah thought as she came in and took her old place on the sofa; for Mary was trying, successfully, to hide her desolation; and as she sat among them in their quietness it was somewhat diminished. After all, she told herself, he *was there*. More strongly even than when he was here in the room with me. Anyhow. And she was grateful for their silence.

Finally Andrew said, "Aunt Hannah has an idea about it, Mary."

"Maybe you'd prefer not to talk about it," Hannah said.

"No; it's all right; I guess I'd rather." And with mild surprise she found that this was true.

"Well, it's simply that I thought of all the old tales and beliefs about the souls of people who die sudden deaths, or violent deaths. Or as Joel would prefer it, not souls. Just their life force. Their consciousness. Their life itself."

"Can't get around that," Joel said. "Hannah was saying that everything of any importance leaves the body then. I certainly have to agree with that."

"And that even whether you believe or not in life after

death," Mary said, "in the soul, as a living, immortal thing, creature, why it's certainly very believable that for a little while afterwards, this force, this life, stays on. Hovers around."

"Sounds highly unlikely to me, but I suppose it's conceivable."

"Like looking at a light and then shutting your eyes. No, not like that but—but it does stay on. Specially when it's someone very strong, very vital, who hasn't been worn down by old age, or a long illness or something."

"That's exactly it," Andrew said. "Something that comes out whole, because it's so quick."

"Why they're as old as the hills, those old beliefs."

"I should imagine they're as old as life and death," Andrew said.

"The thing I mean is, they aren't taken straight to God," Hannah said. "They've had such violence done them, such a shock, it takes a while to get their wits together."

"That's why it took him so long to come," Mary said. "As if his very *soul* had been struck unconscious."

"I should think maybe."

"And above all with someone like Jay, young, and with children and a wife, and not even dreaming of such a thing coming on him, no time to adjust his mind and feelings, or prepare for it."

"That's just it," Andrew said; Hannah nodded.

"Why he'd feel, 'I'm worried. This came too fast without warning. There are all kinds of things I've got to tend to. I can't just leave them like this.' *Wouldn't* HE! And that's just how he was, how we felt he was. So *an*xious. So awfully concerned, and disturbed. Why yes, it's just exactly the way it was!

"And only when they feel convinced you know they care, and everything's going to be taken good care of, just the very best possible, it's only then they can stop being anxious and begin to rest."

They nodded and for a minute they were all quiet.

Then Mary said tenderly, "How awful, pitiful, beyond

words it must be, to be so terribly anxious for others, for others' good, and not be able to do anything, even to say so. Not even to help. Poor things.

"Oh they *do* need reassuring. They *do* need rest. I'm *so* *grateful* I could assure him. It's so good he can rest at last. I'm *so glad.*" And her heart was restored from its desolation, into warmth and love and almost into wholeness.

Emily Brontë
1818–1848

Heathcliff, the demonic hero of *Wuthering Heights*, must be counted as one of literature's least successful mourners. His eighteen-year search for his dead Catherine is a novelistic illumination of the quest of the mourner who has invested too much of his identity in another human being.

Although Catherine and Heathcliff believe each is the other's soul, she marries Edgar Linton and dies after giving birth to Linton's child, telling Heathcliff that she will take him with her. He commands her to haunt him in any form, not leave him in an abyss where he cannot find her.

For eighteen years she haunts him across the moors. After Catherine's gravesite is opened for the burial of Linton, Heathcliff tells the housekeeper Nelly of his macabre reunion with his dead love.

---

from *Wuthering Heights*

"I'll tell you what I did yesterday! I got the sexton, who was digging Linton's grave, to remove the earth off her coffin-lid, and I opened it. I thought, once, I would have stayed there, when I saw her face again—it is hers yet—he had hard work to stir me; but he said it would change, if the air blew on it, and so I struck one side of the coffin loose, and covered it up—not Linton's side, damn him! I wish he'd been soldered in lead—and I bribed the sexton to pull it away, when I'm laid there, and slide mine out too. I'll have it made so, and then, by the time Linton gets to us, he'll not know which is which!"

"You were very wicked, Mr. Heathcliff!" I exclaimed; "were you not ashamed to disturb the dead?"

"I disturbed nobody, Nelly," he replied, "and I gave some ease to myself. I shall be a great deal more comfortable now; and you'll have a better chance of keeping me underground, when I get there. Disturbed her? No! she has disturbed me, night and day, through eighteen years—incessantly—remorselessly—till yesternight; and yesternight I was tranquil. I dreamt I was sleeping the last sleep by that sleeper, with my heart stopped and my cheek frozen against hers."

"And if she had been dissolved into earth, or worse, what would you have dreamt of then?" I said.

"Of dissolving with her, and being more happy still!" he answered. "Do you suppose I dread any change of that sort? I expected such a transformation on raising the lid, but I'm better pleased that it should not commence till I share it. Besides, unless I had received a distinct impression of her passionless features, that strange feeling would hardly have been removed. It began oddly. You know, I was wild after she died, and eternally, from dawn to dawn, praying her to return to me—her spirit— I have a strong faith in ghosts; I have a conviction that they can, and do exist, among us!

"The day she was buried, there came a fall of snow. In the evening I went to the churchyard. It blew bleak as winter—all round was solitary; I didn't fear that her fool of a husband would wander up the den so late, and no one else had business to bring them there.

"Being alone, and conscious two yards of loose earth was the sole barrier between us, I said to myself—

" 'I'll have her in my arms again! If she be cold, I'll think it

is this north wind that chills *me*; and if she be motionless, it is
sleep.'

"I got a spade from the toolhouse, and began to delve with
all my might—it scraped the coffin; I fell to work with my
hands; the wood commenced cracking about the screws, I was
on the point of attaining my object, when it seemed that I heard
a sigh from someone above, close at the edge of the grave, and
bending down. 'If I can only get this off,' I muttered, 'I wish they
may shovel in the earth over us both!' and I wrenched more des-
perately still. There was another sigh, close at my ear. I appeared
to feel the warm breath of it displacing the sleet-laden wind. I
knew no living thing in flesh and blood was by; but as certainly
as you perceive the approach to some substantial body in the
dark, though it cannot be discerned, so certainly I felt that Cathy
was there: not under me, but on the earth.

"A sudden sense of relief flowed, from my heart, through
every limb. I relinquished my labour of agony, and turned consoled at once, unspeakably consoled. Her presence was with me;
it remained while I re-filled the grave, and led me home. You
may laugh, if you will, but I was sure I should see her there. I
was sure she was with me, and I could not help talking to her.

"Having reached the Heights, I rushed eagerly to the door.
It was fastened; and, I remember, that accursed Earnshaw and
my wife opposed my entrance. I remember stopping to kick the
breath out of him, and then hurrying upstairs, to my room, and
hers. I looked round impatiently—I felt her by me—I could
almost see her, and yet I *could not*! I ought to have sweat blood
then, from the anguish of my yearning—from the fervour of
my supplications to have but one glimpse! I had not one. She
showed herself, as she often was in life, a devil to me! And, since
then, sometimes more and sometimes less, I've been the sport
of that intolerable torture! Infernal—keeping my nerves at such
a stretch, that, if they had not resembled catgut, they would,
long ago, have relaxed to the feebleness of Linton's.

"When I sat in the house with Hareton, it seemed that on
going out, I should meet her; when I walked on the moors I

should meet her coming in. When I went from home, I hastened to return—she *must* be somewhere at the Heights, I was certain! And when I slept in her chamber—I was beaten out of that—I couldn't lie there; for the moment I closed my eyes, she was either outside the window, or sliding back the panels, or entering the room, or even resting her darling head on the same pillow as she did when a child. And I must open my lids to see. And so I opened and closed them a hundred times a night—to be always disappointed! It racked me! I've often groaned aloud, till that old rascal Joseph no doubt believed that my conscience was playing the fiend inside of me.

"Now, since I've seen her, I'm pacified—a little. It was a strange way of killing, not by inches, but by fractions of hairbreadths, to beguile me with the spectre of a hope, through eighteen years!"

Pearl Buck
1892–1973

After her husband's death, Pearl Buck went to Japan to work on a film based on one of her books. Work absorbed her during the days, but during her solitary nights in a hotel room she was preoccupied with a search for his presence.

from *A Bridge for Passing*

How incredible, above all, that for the whole first half of my life, I did not know he existed! When I was here before, where was he? And now when I am here again, where now is he? Between these two eras were twenty-five good years of life together, a gem set into eternity before and after. And the old question beset me again, as it besets every human being who has known death come too near. I set my teeth against the inexorability of death.

Is there life beyond?

I remembered the courage of his atheism. How often we argued of the future in which one of us must live alone! For it would have been too good to be possible that we should die at the same moment and hand in hand cross the invincible barrier. I had known for years that it would be I who would be left, I with the heritage of long-living ancestors on both sides of my family. The question was should I remind myself of the possibility of life beyond or thrust it aside and live as though eternity were now—which it is, in one sense, there being no beginning or end in the endlessness of all things. So what then is the present solitude in which I am living? Is it an end to what once was, or is it a beginning to something I do not yet comprehend?

Did he know I was here in Japan? Was he still hovering about the house at home, the essence of himself, and were I there would I perceive his presence? Lying there on my Japanese bed, the sound of the rising sea mingling with the rain on the tiled roof, I fought off the mighty yearning to go in search of him, wherever he was. For surely he was looking for me, too. We were ill at ease, always, when apart. But what are the pathways?

[After the premiere of her film, she feels the realization of an artist whose imagination has given birth to a character who is alive for others. She longs to share the moment with someone, but the hundreds of people crowding around her are strangers. She walks away through the darkness and is driven back to her hotel.]

In that moment I realized what before I had only known. He was dead. There was to be no further communication. Had communication been possible it would have come by some means out there in darkness when I was alone in the crowd. He would have heard me, he would have known my need. Whatever the barriers, he would have found the way to me somehow, had he been awake and aware, wherever he was. He had always found a way. That he did not could only mean that communication was now impossible or that he was neither awake nor aware.

The hotel room became intolerable again. I slipped unseen through empty corridors and walked the silent streets of the town. All decent folk were in bed, and even a drunken man was staggering his way home. The moon was full—somehow a month had passed—and by its light I left the town and went out into the country. Silence, silence everywhere and only silence, because death is silence. I do not know how long I walked or how far, or even where, except it was beside the sea, so calm that there were no waves, only the long swell of the deep tides. I remember how beautiful the landscape was, by night, the mountains rising above silver mists in the valleys. I saw everything and felt nothing. It was as though I were floating and far away, in a strange country in which I had no life. I might have been dead myself, so profound was the silence within. I would never weep again. I knew now there was no use in tears, nor any comfort to be sought or found. There was only this one— myself. Silly to cry for myself!

I turned inland from the sea then and was walking along a narrow path between rice fields. The air was windless until suddenly a wind rose from nowhere, it seemed, and I stopped to feel the freshness on my face. At that same moment I heard a child cry, a baby, I could tell by the high frantic agony. I looked about me. Yes, a farmhouse across the field was bright with lights. Was the child ill? I have heard so many babies cry that I know their language. No, this was not agony—surprise, perhaps, fear, even anger. It was the cry of a newborn child.

I sank down on the grassy bank, listening. The crying stopped, and I heard voices and laughter. The child was a boy, then! The child was another life. I lay back on the grass as though upon a bed and for a long time gazed up into the sky. The stars were not visible, for the bright moon was swinging its arc across the heavens and I watched it until I could believe I saw it move. A desperate weariness was creeping into my bones, the weariness of acceptance, the acceptance of the inescapable, the conviction of the unchangeable. From now on I must never again expect to share the great moments of my life. There would be such moments as long as I was alive, moments of beauty, moments of excitement and exhilaration; above all, moments of achievement. In such moments he and I had turned to each other as instinctively as we breathed. That was no more to be . . . It is not true that one never walks alone. There is an eternity where one walks alone and we do not know its end.

The night was over and in the east beneath the horizon the sun was shining. It was time to go back to my room, time to prepare for the day's work.

R. K. Narayan

Narayan lost his young wife in 1939 after five years of marriage. The hero of his partly autobiographical novel is a teacher of English in India whose wife, Susila, dies. For several months he tries to communicate with her spirit.

from *The English Teacher*

I was walking down our lone street late at night, enveloped in the fragrance of the jasmine and rose garland, slung on my arm. "For whom I am carrying this jasmine home?" I asked myself. Susila would treasure a garland for two whole days, cutting up and sticking masses of it in her hair morning and evening. "Carrying a garland to a lonely house—a dreadful job," I told myself.

I fumbled with the key in the dark, opened the door and switched on the light. I hung up the garland on a nail and kicked up the roll of bedding. The fragrance permeated the whole house. I sprinkled a little water on the flowers to keep them fresh, put out the light and lay down to sleep.

The garland hung by the nail right over my head. The few drops of water which I sprinkled on the flowers seemed to have quickened in them a new life. Their essences came forth into the dark night as I lay in bed, bringing a new vigour with them. The atmosphere became surcharged with strange spiritual forces. Their delicate aroma filled every particle of the air, and as I let my mind float in the ecstasy, gradually perceptions and senses deepened. Oblivion crept over me like a cloud. The past, present and the future welded into one.

I had been thinking of the day's activities and meetings and associations. But they seemed to have no place now. I checked my mind. Bits of memory came floating—a gesture of Brown's, the toy house in the dentist's front room, Rangappa with a garland, and the ring of many speeches and voices—all this was gently overwhelmed and swept aside, till one's mind became clean and bare and a mere chamber of fragrance. It was a superb, noble intoxication. And I had no choice but to let my mind and memories drown in it. I softly called "Susila! Susila, my wife . . ." with all my being. It sounded as if it were a hypnotic melody. "My wife . . . my wife, my wife. . . ." My mind trembled with this rhythm, I forgot myself and my own existence. I fell into a drowse, whispering, "My wife, wife." How long? How could I say? When I opened my eyes again she was sitting on my bed looking at me with an extraordinary smile in her eyes.

"Susila! Susila!" I cried. "You here!" "Yes, I'm here, have always been here." I sat up leaning on my pillow. "Why do you disturb yourself?" she asked.

"I am making a place for you," I said, edging away a little. I looked her up and down and said: "How well you look!" Her complexion had a golden glow, her eyes sparkled with a new light, her saree shimmered with blue interwoven with "light" as she had termed it. . . . "How beautiful!" I said looking at it. "Yes, I always wear this when I come to you. I know you like it very much," she said. I gazed on her face. There was an overwhelming fragrance of jasmine surrounding her. "Still jasmine-scented!" I commented.

"Oh wait," I said and got up. I picked up the garland from the nail and returned to bed. I held it to her. "For you as ever. I somehow feared you wouldn't take it. . . ." She received it with a smile, cut off a piece of it and stuck it in a curve on the back of her head. She turned her head and asked: "Is this all right?"

"Wonderful," I said, smelling it.

A cock crew. The first purple of the dawn came through our window, and faintly touched the walls of our room. "Dawn!" she whispered and rose to her feet.

We stood at the window, gazing on a slender, red streak over the eastern rim of the earth. A cool breeze lapped our faces. The boundaries of our personalities suddenly dissolved. It was a moment of rare, immutable joy—a moment for which one feels grateful to Life and Death.

William Maxwell

from *Ancestors*

It is not true that the dead desert the living. They go away for a very short time, and then they come back and stay as long as they are needed. But sooner or later a time comes when they are in the way; their presence is, for one reason or another, an embarrassment; there is no place for them in the lives of those they once meant everything to. Then they go away for good.

When I was in college I was wakened out of a sound sleep by my own voice, answering my mother, who had called to me from the stairs. With my heart pounding, I waited for more and there wasn't any more. Nothing like it ever happened to me before, or since.

Linda Hartman

Hartman writes that when she was left as a young widow with two small children, she did not permit herself time to grieve. Two years after her husband's death she experienced severe anxiety attacks and sought help. She joined a women's group where she learned a technique of guided fantasy in which the subject allows herself to enter a state of receptivity to unconscious images and, in imagination, is led into a specific setting where those images reveal a story of inner truths.

In this selection, she is nearing recovery from her anxiety symptoms. In the safety of the group setting, led by therapist Mary Ellen, she meets Death himself.

---

from *The Day After Death*

I continued to fear the anxiety attacks even though I hadn't had one in months. I never stopped being afraid. . . . I was plagued by the image of being trapped in a tunnel . . . I could see myself entering that dark, dangerous hole, progressing halfway and then being struck with panic. Turning back was as intolerable as continuing; in my indecision I would stand, unable to move, while both ends of the tunnel caved in. I would then either go crazy or be buried alive.

Whenever I drove anywhere in the car, I gauged traffic so I wouldn't be stuck under an overpass. I would only go into a tunnel if I could see the other end. I avoided bridges. I knew that before I left the group there was one last thing I needed to do. Go into the tunnel.

Mary Ellen began the fantasy as she had all the others. She asked me to describe the meadow to her.

"It's a cold, dismal day. The sky is a lifeless grey—it looks as if someone did a poor job of painting it. The grass is prickly and damp and there are no flowers."

"Linda, if you look around, you will notice a path that leads to a tunnel at the edge of the meadow. When you are ready, I want you to walk toward the tunnel."

I saw the tunnel, black and ominous, like the mouth of a serpent. I set my jaw and started moving toward it, filled with resistance and dread.

Suddenly I was being pushed . . . prodded from behind. I tried to stop but the force was much stronger than I was. I turned to face a tall, thin spectre in a black hooded robe. Death.

I screamed, "Stop pushing me! You've pushed me enough! Leave me alone. I'll go into the tunnel in my own time."

I walked on, acutely aware of his silent presence walking beside me toward the tunnel. In his hand was a long, wooden staff, curved at the upper end: the shepherd of the dead. I drew into myself as much as I could. How I loathed him. He'd been with me all my life, snatching people from me, waiting for me to make a wrong move. Only my cunning had kept me from him. He matched my step.

I reached the entrance and without hesitating, stepped into the blackness. I felt like Alice in Wonderland, falling down, down, with a sort of absent-minded awareness that this was not a tunnel at all. My fall ended abruptly. . . .

Before me was another meadow, much the same as the first one. Across it gaped another black hole, the tunnel I was seeking. This time I walked through the field more resolutely. I entered the black space and found a place all too familiar.

Not far from the house where I lived as a child, there was an underpass under the railroad tracks to the other side of the highway. Many stories were told about "The Underpass" and broken glass and blood stains substantiated the grim tales. I used to run when I went through it, the stale air cold against my bare legs.

"I'm in the tunnel. I don't like it here," I told Mary Ellen. "I want to run as fast as I can and get out of here."

"Why don't you do that?" she asked.

"I'm afraid if I start running, the far end of the tunnel will collapse."

"Start running, Linda, and see what happens."

I bolted toward the distant opening but realized my effort was futile. I watched as the tunnel caved in. I turned, only to see the entrance crash down as well. I was caught in the tunnel with Death!

Small lights along the wall gave enough illumination to see him standing next to me. He seemed unconcerned about the turn of events and sat down calmly on the cold pavement.

"I don't believe it," I told Mary Ellen. "Death just sat down. He acts as if he's on a picnic.

"Get away," I screamed. "I don't want you near me."

His movements slow and heavy, he stood up. He bent and kissed me gently on the top of my head, then turned and walked resignedly to the end of the tunnel and sat down in the rubble.

I told Mary Ellen, "He looks so pathetic, sitting there, lonely, shunned by all living things."

Death seemed transformed from an invincible force into a pitiable creature, tired and beaten. Even I had intimidated him. I felt sorry for him; suddenly, he was the victim.

I rationalized to Mary Ellen, "He's only doing his job. It isn't *his* fault the universe is set up the way it is." I knew it sounded absurd; nevertheless, I walked to him and asked him to rejoin me.

As we walked together toward the middle of the tunnel, the far end began to open. I could see daylight. The entrance opened. The tunnel was no longer a trap.

I told Mary Ellen, "The tunnel is spreading, growing wider and higher. Cars are driving through from one side to the other—it's now a main thoroughfare."

Houses appeared, streets, sidewalks, lawns. People walked there, children played and laughed. A community grew in seconds.

Death stood taking it all in. He seemed as surprised as I

was. His appearance changed. I told Mary Ellen, "His robe has turned from black to a lovely striped pattern—red, blue, green, gold, purple and orange. It's a splendid garment, full of life. He looks relaxed and happy."

"Ask him what the fantasy means. What's the significance of the tunnel?"

Death said, "Your life has been too narrow. It is time for you to expand and grow."

"What about the anxiety attacks? How can I go around expanding when I can't even leave town?"

"You need not worry about them any more," he assured me. He raised his staff and it contracted, magically, until it was only four inches long, and then handed it to me. I found that I was holding a bamboo key chain.

"Take this with you," he said, "as a reminder of your own power. You can control the anxiety."

"Do you want anything else from him?" Mary Ellen asked. "No."

I walked back to the meadow, to the room.

"Death is so ordinary," I told her. "Sort of like your next door neighbor. I don't think he's very happy in his work."

The Reassurances of the Dead

Perhaps to reassure themselves in their own mourning process, over the centuries poets have assumed the persona of the dead, acknowledging that they will fade in the memory of the mourners and counseling them to get on with their own lives.

Anonymous English Ballad
Fifteenth to Sixteenth Century

The Unquiet Grave

"The wind doth blow to-day, my love,
    And a few small drops of rain;
I never had but one true-love,
    In cold grave she was lain.

"I'll do as much for my true-love
    As any young man may;
I'll sit and mourn all at her grave,
    For a twelve month and a day."

The twelve month and a day being up,
    The dead began to speak:
"O who sits weeping on my grave,
    And will not let me sleep?"

" 'Tis I my love, sits on your grave,
    And I will not let you sleep;

For I crave one kiss of your clay-cold lips,
    And that is all I seek."

"You crave one kiss of my clay-cold lips;
    But my breath smells earthy strong;
If you have one kiss of my clay-cold lips,
    Your time will not be long.

" 'Tis down in yonder garden green,
    Love, where we used to walk,
The finest flower that ere was seen
    Is withered to a stalk.

"The stalk is withered dry, my love,
    So will our hearts decay;
So make your self content, my love,
    Till God calls you away."

Christina Rossetti
1830–1894

Remember

Remember me when I am gone away,
Gone far away into the silent land;
When you can no more hold me by the hand,
Nor I half turn to go, yet turning stay.
Remember me when no more, day by day,
You tell me of our future that you planned:
Only remember me; you understand
It will be late to counsel then or pray.
Yet it you should forget me for a while
And afterwards remember, do not grieve:

For if the darkness and corruption leave
A vestige of the thoughts that once I had,
Better by far you should forget and smile
Than that you should remember and be sad.

William Shakespeare
1564–1616

Sonnet LXXI

No longer mourn for me when I am dead
Than you shall hear the surly sullen bell
Give warning to the world that I am fled
From this vile world, with vilest worms to dwell:
Nay, if you read this line, remember not
The hand that writ it; for I love you so
That I in your sweet thoughts would be forgot
If thinking on me then should make you woe.
O, if, I say, you look upon this verse
When I perhaps compounded am with clay,
Do not so much as my poor name rehearse,
But let your love even with my life decay,
    Lest the wise world should look into your moan
    And mock you with me after I am gone.

Grief's Wisdom

To pass through mourning is to emerge into a new reality. The next writers speak to the hard-won education that grief provides. Their insights may not be welcome early in the mourning process and perhaps can be absorbed only after we ourselves have changed.

William Dean Howells
1837–1920

from *The Rise of Silas Lapham*

Many burdened souls . . . bowed down with the only misery like theirs in the universe; for each one of us must suffer long to himself before he can learn that he is but one in a great community of wretchedness which has been pitilessly repeating itself from the foundations of the world.

THE HOLY BIBLE
(King James Version)

from the Book of Ecclesiastes (2:18)

For in much wisdom is much grief: and he that increaseth knowledge increaseth sorrow.

Albert Camus
1913–1960

from *Youthful Writings*

But the astonishing or unfortunate thing is that these deprivations bring us the cure at the same time that they give rise to
pain. Once we have accepted the fact of loss, we understand that
the loved one obstructed a whole corner of the possible, pure
now as a sky washed by rain. Freedom emerges from weariness.
To be happy is to stop. Free, we seek anew, enriched by pain.
And the perpetual impulse forward always falls back again to
gather new strength. The fall is brutal, but we set out again.

Rainer Maria Rilke
1875–1926

from *Letters to a Young Poet*

"You have had many and great sadnesses, which passed. And
you say that even this passing was hard for you and put you out
of sorts. But, please, consider whether these great sadnesses have
not rather gone right through the center of yourself? Whether
much in you has not altered, whether you have not somewhere,
at some point of your being, undergone a change while you
were sad? Only those sadnesses are dangerous and bad which
one carries about among people in order to drown them out;
like sicknesses that are superficially and foolishly treated they
simply withdraw and after a little pause break out again the
more dreadfully; and accumulate within one and are life, are
unlived, spurned, lost life, of which one may die. Were it possible for us to see further than our knowledge reaches, and yet a
little way beyond the outworks of our divining, perhaps we

would endure our sadnesses with greater confidence than our joys. For they are the moments when something new has entered into us, something unknown; our feelings grow mute in shy perplexity, everything in us withdraws, a stillness comes, and the new, which no one knows, stands in the midst of it and is silent."

Albert Camus
1913–1960

from *Notebooks 1942–1951*

Death gives its shape to love as it does to life—transforming it into fate. The one you love died while you loved her and now it is a love fixed forever—which, without such an end, would have fallen to pieces. What would the world be without death—a succession of forms evaporating and returning, an anguished flight, an unfinishable world. But fortunately here is death, the stable one. And the lover weeping over the beloved's remains, René beside Pauline, sheds the tears of pure joy—with the feeling that all is finished—of the man who finally recognizes that his fate has taken shape.

Algernon Charles Swinburne
1837–1909

from The Garden of Prosperine

From too much love of living,
   From hope and fear set free,
We thank with brief thanksgiving

Whatever gods may be
That no life lives for ever;
That dead men rise up never;
That even the weariest river
  Winds somewhere safe to sea.

Walt Whitman
1819–1892

from *Song of Myself*

All goes onward and outward, nothing collapses,
And to die is different from what any one supposed,
and luckier. . . .

They are alive and well somewhere,
The smallest sprout shows there is really no death,
And if there ever was, it led forward life, and does not
wait at the end to arrest it,
And ceas'd the moment life appear'd.

Time and Acquiescence

Conventional wisdom has it that time heals all wounds. The writers in this concluding section express how complicated and individual mending is; the time required for healing cannot be measured against any fixed calendar. They suggest that sorrow does not end, but is transformed into a heightened awareness of life's meaning.

Mary Lavin in her short story "In a Café" probes feelings that are rarely spoken of, including a middle-aged widow's stab of envy for a younger widow's situation. Linda Pastan takes the psychological construct of "stages" of grief and with irony bends the theory to describe not a linear progression but the circularity of her own path to acceptance.

Time's gift to the living is that we are able to move on and grow. To honor the dead is to expand the legacy they left us of themselves, as Michele Murray honors her grandmother after a dozen years of death, and Sharon Olds her lover of twenty years before. He remains forever fixed in youth while she lives for them both the full life their young love promised.

May Sarton affirms that those we have loved are an inextricable part of us. We are their voices. This tenderness is radiant in John Hall Wheelock's tragic yet serene vision in old age of the redeeming value of life.

J. V. Cunningham

from Epigrams

Time heals not: it extends a sorrow's scope
As goldsmiths gold, which we may wear like hope.

Mary Tighe
1772–1810

To Time

Yes, gentle Time, thy gradual, healing hand
   Hath stolen from sorrow's grasp the envenomed dart;
   Submitting to thy skill, my passive heart
Feels that no grief can thy soft power withstand;
   And though my aching breast still heaves the sigh,
   Though oft the tear swells silent in mine eye;
Yet the keen pang, the agony is gone;
   Sorrow and I shall part; and these faint throes
   Are but the remnant of severer woes:
As when the furious tempest is o'erblown,
   And when the sky has wept its violence,
The opening heavens will oft let fall a shower,
   The poor o'ercharged boughs still drops dispense,
And still the loaded streams in torrents pour.

Sophocles
496–406 B.C.

from *Ajax*

The happiest life consists in ignorance,
Before you learn to grieve and to rejoice.

Mary Lavin

In a Café

The café was in a back street. Mary's ankles ached and she was glad Maudie had not got there before her. She sat down at a table near the door.

It was a place she had only recently found, and she dropped in often, whenever she came up to Dublin. She hated to go anywhere else now. For one thing, she knew that she would be unlikely ever to have set foot in it if Richard were still alive. And this knowledge helped to give her back a semblance of the identity she lost willingly in marriage, but lost doubly, and unwillingly, in widowhood.

Not that Richard would have disliked the café. It was the kind of place they went to when they were students. Too much water had gone under the bridge since those days, though. Say what you liked, there was something faintly snobby about a farm in Meath, and together she and Richard would have been out of place here. But it was a different matter to come here alone. There could be nothing—oh, nothing—snobby about a widow. Just by being one, she fitted into this kind of café. It was an unusual little place. She looked around.

The walls were distempered red above and the lower part was boarded, with the boards painted white. It was probably the boarded walls that gave it the peculiarly functional look you get in the snuggery of a public-house or in the confessional of a small and poor parish church. For furniture there were only deal tables and chairs, with black-and-white checked tablecloths that were either unironed or badly ironed. But there was a decided feeling that money was not so much in short supply as dedicated to other purposes—as witness the paintings on the walls, and a notice over the fire-grate to say that there were others on view in a studio overhead, in rather the same way as pictures in an exhibition. They were for the most part experimental in their technique.

The café was run by two students from the Art College. They often went out and left the place quite empty—as now—while they had a cup of coffee in another café—across the street. Regular clients sometimes helped themselves to coffee from the pot on the gas-ring, behind a curtain at the back; or, if they only came in for company and found none, merely warmed themselves at the big fire always blazing in the little black grate that was the original grate when the café was a warehouse office. Today, the fire was banked up with coke. The coffee was spitting on the gas-ring.

Would Maudie like the place? That it might not be exactly the right place to have arranged to meet her, above all under the present circumstances, occurred vaguely to Mary, but there was nothing that could be done about it now. When Maudie got there, if she didn't like it, they could go somewhere else. On the other hand, perhaps she might like it? Or perhaps she would be too upset to take notice of her surroundings? The paintings might interest her. They were certainly stimulating. There were two new ones today, which Mary herself had not seen before: two flower paintings, just inside the door. From where she sat she could read the signature, Johann van Stiegler. Or at least they suggested flowers. They were nameable as roses surely in spite of being a bit angular. She knew what Richard would have said about them. But she and Richard were no longer one. So what would *she* say about them? She would say—she would say—

But what was keeping Maudie? It was all very well to be glad of a few minutes' time in which to gather herself together; it was a different thing altogether to be kept a quarter of an hour.

Mary leaned back against the boarding. She was less tired than when she came in, but she was still in no way prepared for the encounter in front of her.

What had she to say to a young widow recently bereaved? Why on earth had she arranged to meet her? The incongruity of their both being widowed came forcibly upon her. Would

Maudie, too, be in black with touches of white? Two widows! It was like two magpies: one for sorrow, two for joy. The absurdity of it was all at once so great she had an impulse to get up and make off out of the place. She felt herself vibrating all over with resentment at being coupled with anyone, and urgently she began to sever them, seeking out their disparities.

Maudie was only a year married! And her parents had been only too ready to take care of her child, greedily possessing themselves of it. Maudie was as free as a girl. Then—if it mattered—?—she had a nice little income in her own right too, apart from all Michael had left her. So?

But what was keeping her? Was she not coming at all?

Ah! the little iron bell that was over the door—it too, since the warehouse days—tinkled to tell there was another customer coming into the café.

It wasn't Maudie though. It was a young man—youngish anyway—and Mary would say that he was an artist. Yet his hands at which, when he sat down, he began to stare, were not like the hands of an artist. They were peculiarly plump soft-skinned hands, and there was something touching in the relaxed way in which, lightly clasped one in the other, they rested on the table. Had they a womanish look perhaps? No; that was not the word, but she couldn't for the life of her find the right word to describe them. And her mind was teased by trying to find it. Fascinated, her eyes were drawn to those hands, time and again, no matter how resolutely she tore them away. It was almost as if it was by touch, not sight, that she knew their warm fleshiness.

Even when she closed her eyes—as she did—she could still see them. And so, innocent of where she was being led, she made no real effort to free her thoughts from them, and not until it was too late did she see before her the familiar shape of her recurring nightmare. All at once it was Richard's hands she saw, so different from those others, wiry, supple, thin. There they were for an instant in her mind, limned by love and anguish, before they vanished.

It happened so often. In her mind she would see a part of him, his hand—his arm, his foot perhaps, in the finely worked leather shoes he always wore—and from it, frantically, she would try to build up the whole man. Sometimes she succeeded better than others, built him up from foot to shoulder, seeing his hands, his grey suit, his tie, knotted always in a slightly special way, his neck, even his chin that was rather sharp, a little less attractive than his other features—

—But always at that point she would be defeated. Never once voluntarily since the day he died had she been able to see his face again.

And if she could not remember him, at will, what meaning had time at all? What use was it to have lived the past, if behind us it fell away so sheer?

In the hour of his death, for her it was part of the pain that she knew this would happen. She was standing beside him when, outside the hospital window, a bird called out with a sweet, clear whistle, and hearing it she knew that he was dead, because not for years had she really heard bird-song or bird-call, so loud was the noise of their love in her ears. When she looked down it was a strange face, the look of death itself, that lay on the pillow. And after that brief moment of silence that let in the bird-song for an instant, a new noise started in her head; the noise of a nameless panic that did not always roar, but never altogether died down.

And now—here in the little café—she caught at the table-edge—for the conflagration had started again and her mind was a roaring furnace.

It was just then the man at the end of the table stood up and reached for the menu-card on which, as a matter of fact, she was leaning—breasts and elbows—with her face in her hands. Hastily, apologetically, she pushed it towards him, and at once the roar died down in her mind. She looked at him. Could he have known? Her heart was filled with gratitude, and she saw that his eyes were soft and gentle. But she had to admit that he didn't look as if he were much aware of her. No matter! She still was grateful to him.

'Don't you want this too?' she cried, thankful, warm, as she saw that the small slip of paper with the specialty for the day that had been clipped to the menu card with a paper-pin, had come off and remained under her elbow, caught on the rough sleeve of her jacket. She stood up and leant over the table with it.

'Ah! thank you!' he said, and bowed. She smiled. There was such gallantry in a bow. He was a foreigner, of course. And then, before she sat down again she saw that he had been sketching, making little pencil sketches all over a newspaper on the table, in the margins and in the spaces between the newsprint. Such intricate minutely involuted little figures—she was fascinated, but of course she could not stare.

Yet, when she sat down, she watched him covertly, and every now and then she saw that he made a particular flourish: it was his signature, she felt sure, and she tried to make it out from where she sat. A disproportionate, a ridiculous excitement rushed through her, when she realised it was Johann van Stiegler, the name on the new flower paintings that had preoccupied her when she first came into the place.

But it's impossible, she thought. The sketches were so meticulous; the paintings so—

But the little bell had tinkled again.

'Ah! Maudie!'

For all her waiting, taken by surprise in the end, she got to her feet in her embarrassment, like a man.

'Maudie, my dear!' She had to stare fixedly at her in an effort to convey the sympathy, which, tongue-tied, she could express in no other way.

They shook hands, wordlessly.

'I'm deliberately refraining from expressing sympathy—you know that?' said Mary then, as they sat down at the checkered table.

'Oh, I do!' cried Maudie. And she seemed genuinely appre-

ciative. 'It's so awful trying to think of something to say back!—
Isn't it? It has to come right out of yourself, and sometimes what
comes is something you can't even say out loud when you do
think of it!'

It was so true. Mary looked at her in surprise. Her mind
ran back over the things people had said to her, and the replies.

Them: It's a good thing it wasn't one of the children.

Her: I'd give them all for him.

Them: Time is a great healer.

Her: Thief would be more like: taking away even my
memory of him.

Them: God's ways are wonderful. Some day you'll see His
plan in all this.

Her: Do you mean, some day I'll be glad he's dead?

So Maudie apprehended these subtleties too? Mary looked hard
at her. 'I know, I know,' she said. 'In the end you have to say
what is expected of you—and you feel so cheapened by it.'

'Worse still, you cheapen the dead!' said Maudie.

Mary looked really hard at her now. Was it possible for a
young girl—a simple person at that—to have wrung from one
single experience so much bitter knowledge? In spite of herself, she felt she was being drawn into complicity with her. She
drew back resolutely.

'Of course, you were more or less expecting it, weren't you?'
she said, spitefully.

Unrepulsed, Maudie looked back at her. 'Does that matter?'
she asked, and then, unexpectedly, she herself put a rift between
them. 'You have the children, of course!' she said, and then,
hastily, before Mary could say anything, she rushed on. 'Oh, I
know I have my baby, but there seems so little link between
him and his father! I just can't believe that it's me, sometimes,
wheeling him round the park in his pram: it's like as if he was
illegitimate. No! I mean it really. I'm not just trying to be
shocking. It must be so different when there has been time for
a relationship to be started between children and their father,
like there was in your case.'

'Oh, I don't know that that matters,' said Mary. 'And you'll be glad to have him some day.' This time she spoke with deliberate malice, for she knew so well how those same words had lacerated her. She knew what they were meant to say: the children would be better than nothing.

But the poison of her words did not penetrate Maudie. And with another stab she knew why this was so. Maudie was so young; so beautiful. Looking at her, it seemed quite inaccurate to say that she had lost her husband: it was Michael who had lost her, fallen out, as it were, while she perforce went outward. She didn't even look like a widow. There was nothing about her to suggest that she was in any way bereft or maimed.

'You'll marry again, Maudie,' she said, impulsively. 'Don't mind my saying it,' she added quickly, hastily. 'It's not a criticism. It's because I know how you're suffering that I say it. Don't take offence.'

Maudie didn't really look offended though, she only looked on the defensive. Then she relaxed.

'Not coming from you,' she said. 'You know what it's like.' Mary saw she was trying to cover up the fact that she simply could not violently refute the suggestion. 'Not that I think I will,' she added, but weakly. 'After all, you didn't!'

It was Mary who was put upon the defensive now.

'After all, it's only two years—less even,' she said stiffly.

'Oh, it's not altogether a matter of time,' said Maudie, seeing she had erred, but not clear how or where. 'It's the kind of person you are, I think. I admire you so much! It's what I'd want to be like myself if I had the strength. With remarriage it is largely the effect on oneself that matters I think, don't you? I don't think it really matters to—to the dead! Do you? I'm sure Michael would want me to marry again if he were able to express a wish. After all, people say it's a compliment to a man if his widow marries again, did you ever hear that?'

'I did,' said Mary, curtly. 'But I wouldn't pay much heed to it. A fat lot of good the dead care about compliments.'

So Maudie *was* really thinking about remarriage? Mary's

irritation was succeeded by a vague feeling of envy, and then the irritation returned tenfold.

How easily it was accepted that *she* would not marry again. This girl regards me as too old, of course. And she's right—or she ought to be right! She remembered the way, even two years ago, people had said she "had" her children. They meant, even then, that it was unlikely, unlooked for, that she'd remarry.

Other things that had been said crowded back into her mind as well. So many people had spoken of the special quality of her marriage—her's and Richard's—their remarkable suitability one for the other, and the uniqueness of the bond between them. She was avid to hear this said at the time.

But suddenly, in this little café, the light that had played over those words, flickered and went out. Did they perhaps mean that if Richard had not appeared when he did, no one else would have been interested in her?

Whereas Maudie—! If she looked so attractive now, when she must still be suffering from shock, what would she be like a year from now, when she would be "out of mourning," as it would be put? Why, right now, she was so fresh and—looking at her there was no other word for it—virginal! Of course she was only a year married. A year! You could hardly call it being married at all.

But Maudie knew a thing or two about men for all that. There was no denying it. And in her eyes at that moment there was a strange expression. Seeing it, Mary remembered at once that they were not alone in the café. She wondered urgently how much the man at the other end of the table had heard and could hear of what they were saying. But it was too late to stop Maudie.

'Oh Mary,' cried Maudie, leaning forward, 'it's not what they give us—I've got over wanting things like a child—it's what we have to give them! It's something—' and she pressed her hands suddenly to her breasts, 'something in here!'

'Maudie!'

Sharply, urgently, Mary tried to make her lower her voice,

and with a quick movement of her head she did manage at last to convey some caution to her.

'In case you might say something,' she said, in a low voice.

'Oh, there was no fear,' said Maudie. 'I was aware all the time.' She didn't speak quite so low as Mary, but did lower her voice. 'I was aware of him *all the time*,' she said. 'It was *him* that put it into my mind—about what we have to give.' She pressed her hands to her breasts again. 'He looks so lonely, don't you think? He is a foreigner, isn't he? I always think it's sad for them; they don't have many friends, and even when they do, there is always a barrier, don't you agree?'

But Mary was too embarrassed to let her go on. Almost frantically she made a diversion.

'What are you going to have, Maudie?' she said, loudly. 'Coffee? Tea? And is there no one to take an order?'

Immediately she felt a fool. To whom had she spoken? She looked across at Johann van Stiegler. As if he were waiting to meet her glance, his mild and patient eyes looked into her's.

'There is no one there,' he said, nodding at the curtained gas-ring, 'but one can serve oneself. Perhaps you would wish that I—'

'Oh not at all,' cried Mary. 'Please don't trouble! We're in absolutely no hurry! Please don't trouble yourself,' she said, 'not on our account.'

But she saw at once that he was very much a foreigner, and that he was at a disadvantage, not knowing if he had not perhaps made a gaffe. 'I have perhaps intruded?' he said, miserably.

'Oh, not at all,' cried Mary, and he was so serious she had to laugh.

The laugh was another mistake though. His face took on a look of despair that could come upon a foreigner, it seemed, at the slightest provocation, as if suddenly everything was obscure to him—everything.

'Please,' she murmured, and then vaguely, '—your work,' meaning that she did not wish to interrupt his sketching.

'Ah, you know my work?' he said, brightening immediately, pleased and with a small and quite endearing vanity. 'We have met before? Yes?'

'Oh no, we haven't met,' she said, quickly, and she sat down, but of course after that it was impossible to go on acting as if he were a complete stranger. She turned to see what Maudie would make of the situation. It was then she felt the full force of her irritation with Maudie. She could have given her a slap in the face. Yes: a slap right in the face! For there she sat, remotely, her face indeed partly averted from them.

Maudie was waiting to be introduced! To be *introduced*, as if she, Mary, did not need any conventional preliminaries. As if it was all right that she, Mary, should begin an unprefaced conversation with a strange man in a café because—and of course that was what was so infuriating, that she knew Maudie's unconscious thought—it was all right for a woman of *her* age to strike up a conversation like that, but that it wouldn't have done for a young woman. Yet, on her still partly averted face, Mary could see the quickened look of interest. She had a good mind not to make any gesture to draw her into the conversation at all, but she had the young man to consider. She had to bring them together whether she liked it or not.

'Maudie, this is—' she turned back and smiled at van Stiegler, 'this is—' But she was confused and she had to abandon the introduction altogether. Instead, she broke into a direct question.

'Those are your flower pictures, aren't they?' she asked.

It was enough for Maudie—more than enough you might say.

She turned to the young man, obviously greatly impressed; her lips apart, her eyes shining. My God, how attractive she was!

'Oh no, not really?' she cried. 'How marvellous of you!'

But Johann van Stiegler was looking at Mary.

'You are sure we have not met before?'

'Oh no, but you were scribbling your signature all over

that newspaper,' she looked around to show it to him, but it had fallen on to the floor.

'Ah yes,' he said, and—she couldn't be certain, of course—but she thought he was disappointed.

'Ah yes, you saw my signature,' he said, flatly. He looked dejected. Mary felt helpless. She turned to Maudie. It was up to her to say something now.

Just then the little warehouse bell tinkled again, and this time it was one of the proprietors who came in, casually, like a client.

'Ah good!' said van Stiegler. 'Coffee,' he called out. Then he turned to Mary. 'Coffee for you too?'

'Oh yes, coffee for us,' said Mary, but she couldn't help wondering who was going to pay for it, and simultaneously she couldn't help noticing the shabbiness of his jacket. Well—they'd see! Meanwhile, she determined to ignore the plate of cakes that was put down with the coffee. And she hoped Maudie would too. She pushed the plate aside as a kind of hint to her, but Maudie leaned across and took a large bun filled with cream.

'Do you mind my asking you something—about your work—?' said Mary.

But Maudie interrupted.

'You are living in Ireland? I mean, you are not just here on a visit?'

There was intimacy and intimacy, and Mary felt nervous in case the young man might resent this question.

'I teach art in a college here,' he said, and he did seem a little surprised, but Mary could see too, that he was not at all displeased. He seemed to settle more comfortably into the conversation.

'It is very good for a while to go to another country,' he said, 'and this country is cheap. I have a flat in the next street to here, and it is very private. If I hang myself from the ceiling, it is all right—nobody knows; nobody cares. That is a good way to live when you paint.'

Mary was prepared to ponder. 'Do you think so?'

Maudie was not prepared to ponder. 'How odd,' she said, shortly, and then she looked at her watch. 'I'll have to go,' she said, inexplicably.

They had finished the coffee. Immediately Mary's thoughts returned to the problem of who was to pay for it. It was a small affair for which to call up all one's spiritual resources, but she felt enormously courageous and determined when she heard herself ask in a loud voice for her bill.

'My bill, please,' she called out, over the sound of spitting coffee on the gas stove.

Johann van Stiegler made no move to ask for his bill, and yet he was buttoning his jacket and folding his newspaper as if to leave too. Would his coffee go on her bill? Mary wondered.

It was all settled, however, in a second. The bill was for two eight-penny coffees, and one bun, and there was no charge for van Stiegler's coffee. He had some understanding with the owners, she supposed. Or perhaps he was not really going to leave then at all?

As they stood up, however, gloved and ready to depart, the young man bowed.

'Perhaps we go the same way?' and they could see he was anxious to be polite.

'Oh, not at all,' they said together, as if he had offered to escort them, and Maudie even laughed openly.

Then there was, of course, another ridiculous situation. Van Stiegler sat down again. Had they been too brusque? Had they hurt his feelings?

Oh, if only he wasn't a foreigner, thought Mary, and she hesitated. Maudie already had her hand on the door.

'I hope I will see some more of your work sometime,' said Mary. It was not a question, merely a compliment.

But van Stiegler sprung to his feet again though.

'Tonight after my classes I am bringing another picture to hang here,' he said. 'You would like to see it? I would be here—' he pulled out a large, old-fashioned watch, '—at ten minutes past nine.'

'Oh, not tonight—I couldn't come back tonight,' said Mary. 'I live in the country, you see,' she said, explaining and excusing herself. 'Another time perhaps? It will be here for how long?'

She wasn't really listening to what he said. She was thinking that he had not asked if Maudie could come. Perhaps it was that, of the two of them, she looked the most likely to buy a picture, whereas Maudie, although in actual fact more likely to do so, looked less so. Or was it that he coupled them so that he thought if one came, both came. Or was it really Maudie he'd like to see again, and that he regarded her as a chaperone? Or was it—?

There was no knowing, however, and so she said good-bye again, and the next minute the little bell had tinkled over the door and they were in the street. In the street they looked at each other.

'Well! if ever there was—' began Maudie, but she didn't get time to finish her sentence. Behind them the little bell tinkled yet again, and their painter was out in the street with them.

'I forgot to give you the address of my flat—it is also my studio,' he said. 'I would be glad to show you my paintings at any time.' He pulled out a notebook and tore out a sheet. 'I will write it down,' he said, concisely. And he did. But when he went to hand it to them, it was Maudie who took it. 'I am nearly always there, except when I am at my classes,' he said. And bowing, he turned and went back into the café.

They dared not laugh until they had walked some distance away, until they turned into the next street in fact.

'Well, I never!' said Maudie, and she handed the paper to Mary.

'Chantham Row,' Mary read, 'number 8.'

'Will you go to see them?' asked Maudie.

Mary felt outraged.

'What do you take me for?' she asked. 'I may be a bit unconventional, but can you see me presenting myself at his place? Would *you* go?'

'Oh, it's different for me,' said Maudie, enigmatically. 'And anyway, it was you he asked. But I see your point—it's a pity. Poor fellow!—he must be very lonely. I wish there was something we could do for him—someone to whom we could introduce him.'

Mary looked at her. It had never occurred to her that he might be lonely! How was it that the obvious always escaped her?

They were in Grafton Street by this time.

'Well, I have some shopping to do. I suppose it's the same with you,' said Maudie. 'I am glad I had that talk with you. We must have another chat soon.'

'Oh yes,' said Mary, over-readily, replying to their adieux though, and not as Maudie thought, to the suggestion of their meeting again! She was anxious all at once to be rid of Maudie.

And yet, as she watched her walk away from her, making her passage quickly and expertly through the crowds in the street, Mary felt a sudden terrible aimlessness descend upon herself like a physical paralysis. She walked along, pausing to look in at the shop windows.

It was the evening hour when everyone in the streets was hurrying home, purposeful and intent. Even those who paused to look into the shop windows did so with direction and aim, darting their bright glances keenly, like birds. Their minds were all intent upon substantives; tangibles, while her mind was straying back to the student café, and the strange flower pictures on the walls; to the young man who was so vulnerable in his vanity: the legitimate vanity of his art.

It was so like Maudie to laugh at him. What did she know of an artist's mind? If Maudie had not been with her, it would have been so different. She might, for one thing, have got him to talk about his work, to explain the discrepancy between the loose style of the pictures on the wall and the exact, small sketches he'd been drawing on the margins of the paper.

She might even have taken up his invitation to go and see his paintings. Why had that seemed so unconventional—so laughable? Because of Maudie, that was why.

How ridiculous their scruples would have seemed to the young man. She could only hope he had not guessed them. She looked up at a clock. Supposing, right now, she were to slip back to the café and suggest that after all she found she would have time for a quick visit to his studio? Or would he have left the café? Better perhaps to call around to the studio? He would surely be back there now!

For a moment she stood debating the arguments for and against going back. Would it seem odd to him? Would he be surprised? But as if it were Maudie who put the questions, she frowned them down and all at once purposeful as anyone in the street, began to go back, headlong, you might say, towards Chatham Street.

At the point where two small streets crossed each other she had to pause, while a team of Guinness's dray horses turned with difficulty in the narrow cube of the intersection. And, while she waited impatiently, she caught sight of herself in the gilded mirror of a public-house. For a second, the familiar sight gave her a misgiving of her mission, but as the dray-horses moved out of the way, she told herself that her dowdy, lumpish, and un-romantic figure vouched for her spiritual integrity. She pulled herself away from the face in the glass and hurried across the street.

Between two lock-up shops, down a short alley—roofed by the second storey of the premises overhead, till it was like a tunnel—was his door. Away at the end of the tunnel the door could clearly be seen even from the middle of the street, for it was painted bright yellow. Odd that she had never seen it in the times she had passed that way. She crossed the street.

Once across the street, she ran down the tunnel, her foot-steps echoing loud in her ears. And there on the door, tied to the latchet of the letter-box, was a piece of white cardboard with his name on it. Grabbing the knocker, she gave three clear hammer-strokes on the door.

The little alley was a sort of cul-de-sac; except for the street behind her and the door in front of her, it had no outlet. There was not even a skylight or an aperture of any kind. As for the premises into which the door led, there was no way of telling its size or its extent, or anything at all about it, until the door was opened.

Irresponsibly, she giggled. It was like the mystifying doors in the trunks of trees that beguiled her as a child in fairy-tales and fantasies. Did this door, too, like those fairy doors, lead into rooms of impossible amplitude, or would it be a cramped and poky place?

As she pondered upon what was within, seemingly so mysteriously sealed, she saw that—just as in a fairy tale—after all there was an aperture. The letter-box had lost its shutter, or lid, and it gaped open, a vacant hole in the wood, reminding her of a sleeping doll whose eyeballs had been poked back in its head, and creating an expression of vacancy and emptiness.

Impulsively, going down on one knee, she peered in through the slit.

And if he opened the door, what then? All the thoughts and words that had, like a wind, blown her down this tunnel, subsided suddenly, and she stood, appalled, at where they had brought her.

'Who iss that?' came the voice within, troubled.

Staring at those white feet, thrust into the unlaced shoes, she felt that she would die on the spot if they moved an inch. She turned.

Ahead of her, bright, shining and clear, as if it were at the end of a powerful telescope, was the street. Not caring if her feet were heard, volleying and echoing as if she ran through a mighty drain-pipe, she kept running till she reached the street, kept running even then, jostling surprised shoppers, hitting her ankles off the wheel-knobs of push-cars and prams. Only when she came to the junction of the streets again, did she stop, as in the pub mirror she caught sight again of her familiar face. That face steadied her. How absurd to think that anyone would sinisterly follow this middle-aged woman?

But suppose he had been in the outer room when she knocked! If he had opened the door? What would have happened then? What would she have said? A flush spread over her face. The only true words that she could have uttered were those that had sunk into her mind in the café; put there by Maudie.

'I'm lonely!' That was all she could have said. 'I'm lonely. Are you?'

A deep shame came over her with this admission and, guiltily, she began to walk quickly onward again, towards Grafton Street. If anyone had seen her, there in that dark alleyway! If anyone could have looked into her mind, her heart!

And yet, was it so unnatural? Was it so hard to understand? So unforgiveable?

As she passed the open door of the Carmelite Church she paused. Could she rid herself of her feeling of shame in the dark of the confessional? To the sin-accustomed ears of wise old fathers her story would be light-weight; a tedious tale of scrupulosity. Was there no one, no one who'd understand?

She had reached Grafton Street once more, and stepped into its crowded thoroughfare. It was only a few minutes since she left it, but in the street the evasion of light had begun. Only the bustle of people, and the activity of traffic, made it seem that it was yet day. Away at the top of the street, in Stephen's Green, to which she turned, although the tops of the trees were still clear, branch for branch, in the last of the light, mist muted the outline of the bushes. If one were to put a hand between the railings now, it would be with a slight shock that the fingers would feel the little branches, like fine bones, under the feathers of mist. And in their secret nests the smaller birds were making faint avowals in the last of the day. It was the time at which she used to meet Richard.

Oh Richard! she cried, almost out loud, as she walked

along by the railings to where the car was parked. Oh Richard! it's you I want.

And as she cried out, her mind presented him to her, as she so often saw him, coming towards her: tall, handsome, and with his curious air of apartness from those around him. He had his hat in his hand, down by his side, as on a summer day he might trail a hand in water from the side of a boat. She wanted to preserve that picture of him forever in an image, and only as she struggled to hold on to it did she realize there was no urgency in the search. She had a sense of having all the time in the world to look and look and look at him. That was the very way he used to come to meet her—indolently trailing the old felt hat, glad to be done with the day; and when they got nearer to each other she used to take such joy in his unsmiling face, with its happiness integral to it in all its features. It was the first time in two years he'd been gone from her that she'd seen his face.

Not till she had taken out the key of the car, and gone straight around to the driver's side, not stupidly, as so often, to the passenger seat—not till then did she realize what she had achieved. Yet she had no more than got back her rights. No more. It was not a subject for amazement. By what means exactly had she got them back though—in that little café? That was the wonder.

Linda Pastan

The Five Stages of Grief

The night I lost you
someone pointed me towards
the Five Stages of Grief.
Go that way, they said,
it's easy, like learning to climb
stairs after the amputation.

And so I climbed.
Denial was first.
I sat down at breakfast
carefully setting the table
for two. I passed you the toast—
you sat there. I passed
you the paper—you hid
behind it.
Anger seemed more familiar.
I burned the toast, snatched
the paper and read the headlines myself.
But they mentioned your departure,
and so I moved on to
Bargaining. What could I exchange
for you? The silence
after storms? My typing fingers?
Before I could decide, *Depression*
came puffing up, a poor relation
its suitcase tied together
with string. In the suitcase
were bandages for the eyes
and bottles of sleep. I slid
all the way down the stairs
feeling nothing.
And all the time Hope
flashed on and off
in defective neon.
Hope was a signpost pointing
straight in the air.
Hope was my uncle's middle name,
he died of it.
After a year I am still climbing,
though my feet slip
on your stone face.
The treeline
has long since disappeared;

green is a color
I have forgotten.
But now I see what I am climbing
towards: *Acceptance*
written in capital letters,
a special headline:
Acceptance,
its name in lights.
I struggle on,
waving and shouting.
Below, my whole life spreads its surf,
all the landscapes I've ever known
or dreamed of. Below
a fish jumps: the pulse
in your neck.
Acceptance. I finally
reach it.
But something is wrong.
Grief is a circular staircase.
I have lost you.

Mary Jane Moffat

In this poem, written almost two years after my husband's death, I think I was struggling with my reluctance to surrender grief and my resentment of well-wishers who urged me away from the past toward the future. Taking the consolers' point of view instead of my own was perhaps a way of reconciling my ambivalence about advice I did not want to hear.

The Passing of Sorrow

At first her grief was a grey
sweater worn under a black

umbrella with broken spokes,
something to hunch under.

Leaning on our proffered arms,
even in the fierce sun
she walked among us
in some darkness of her own.

Our voices low, we left
cakes and wine on her stoop.
Weeks passed; she grew fat
on our sympathy.

Grass healed over his grave.
You are still young, we told her.
In carpet slippers
she showed us to the door.

Thinner now, tanned in a sleeveless
dress, she crosses the street
when she sees us,
shading her eyes.

Charlotte Painter

Charlotte Painter wrote this poem for my husband, an engineer
whose light sources played a part in the 1976 Viking launch
experiments on Mars.

Elegy for Jack Moffat

> "We want to see if corn
> will grow on Mars"

Now Voyager
how do you see—
through pinpoints in the dark
now you are dead?

The Viking ship has gone
from earth, bearing your designs
of light—small fixtures
you called them, modest man.

They were its sun merely.
The space craft moved its sampling
of Martian soil beneath
the tiny perfect source of heat
you made for growing life.

Now Voyager,
go cool as your creations
before that far-red gravity
took them captive, be
free of any orbit,
disengaged from weight.
Have no need of human form,
of its small fixtures
to see all, no need
to send your findings back
through cracks of heavens.

Alfred, Lord Tennyson
1809–1892

from *In Memoriam A.H.H.*

Again at Christmas did we weave
   The holly round the Christmas hearth;
   The silent snow possess'd the earth,
And calmly fell our Christmas-eve.

The yule-log sparkled keen with frost,
   No wing of wind the region swept,
   But over all things brooding slept
The quiet sense of something lost.

As in the winters left behind,
   Again our ancient games had place,
   The mimic picture's breathing grace,
And dance and song and hoodman-blind.

Who show'd a token of distress?
   No single tear, no mark of pain—
   O sorrow, then can sorrow wane?
O grief, can grief be changed to less?

O last regret, regret can die!
   No—mixt with all this mystic frame,
   Her deep relations are the same,
But with long use her tears are dry.

Michele Murray
1934–1974

Poem to My Grandmother in Her Death

After a dozen years of death
even love wanders off, old faithful
dog tired of lying on stiff marble.

In any case you would not understand
this life, the plain white walls
& the books, a passion lost on you.

I do not know what forced your life
through iron years into a shape of giving—
an apple, squares of chocolate, a hand.

There should have been nothing left
after the mean streets, foaming washtubs,
the wild cries of births at home.

Never mind. It's crumbling in my hands,
too, what you gave. I've jumped from ledges
& landed oddly twisted, bleeding internally.

Thus I learn how to remember your injuries—
your sudden heaviness as fine rain fell,
or your silence over the scraped bread board.

Finding myself in the end is finding you
& if you are lost in the folds of your silence
then I find only to lose with you those years

I stupidly flung off me like ragged clothes
when I was ashamed to be the child
of your child. I scrabble for them now

In dark closets because I am afraid.
I have forgotten so much. If I could meet you
again perhaps I could rejoin my own flesh

And not lose whatever you called love.
I could understand your silences & speak them
& you would be as present to me as your worn ring.

In the shadows I reach for the bucket of fierce dahlias
you bought without pricing, the coat you shook
free of its snow, the blouse that you ironed.

There's no love so pure it can thrive
without its incarnations. I would like to know you
once again over your chipped cups brimming with tea.

Sharon Olds

Cambridge Elegy

(FOR HENRY AVERELL GERRY, 1941–1960)

I hardly know how to speak to you now,
you are so young now, closer to my daughter's age
than mine—but I have been there and seen it, and must
tell you, as the seeing and hearing
spell the world into the deaf-mute's hand.
The tiny dormer windows like the ears of a fox, like the
long row of teats on a pig, still
perk up over the Square, though they're digging up the
street now, as if digging a grave,
the shovels shrieking on stone like your car
sliding along on its roof after the crash.
How I wanted everyone to die if you had to die,
how sealed into my own world I was,

deaf and blind. What can I tell you now,
now that I know so much and you are a
freshman still, drinking a quart of orange juice and
playing three sets of tennis to cure a hangover, such an
ardent student of the grown-ups! I can tell you
we were right, our bodies were right, life was
really going to be that good, that
pleasurable in every cell.
Suddenly I remember the exact look of your body, but
better than the bright corners of your eyes, or the
light of your face, the rich Long Island
puppy-fat of your thighs, or the slick
chino of your pants bright in the corners of my eyes, I
remember your extraordinary act of courage in
loving me, something which no one but the
blind and halt had done before. You were
fearless, you could drive after a sleepless night
just like a grown-up, and not be afraid, you could
fall asleep at the wheel easily and
never know it, each blond hair of your head—and they were
thickly laid—put out like a filament of light,
each gold cell of your body stopped like Midas's daughter,
twenty years ago. The Charles still
slides by with that ease that made me bitter when I
wanted all things hard as your death was hard;
wanted all things broken and rigid as the
bricks in the sidewalk or your love for me
stopped cell by cell in your young body.
Ave—I went ahead and had the children,
the life of ease and faithfulness, the
palm and the breast, every millimeter of delight in the body,
I took the road we stood on at the start together, I
took it all without you as if
in taking it after all I could most
honor you.

Mei Shëng and Fu I
First Century B.C.

Years Vanish Like the Morning Dew

I drive my chariot up to the Eastern Gate;
For afar I see the graveyard north of the Wall.
The white aspens how they murmur, murmur;
Pines and cypresses flank the broad paths.
Beneath lie men who died long ago;
Black, black is the long night that holds them.
Deep down beneath the Yellow Springs,
Thousands of years they lie without waking.

In infinite succession light and darkness shift,
And years vanish like the morning dew.
Man's life is like a sojourning,
His longevity lacks the firmness of stone and metal.
For ever it has been that mourners in their turn were mourned,
Saint and Sage,—all alike are trapped.
Seeking by food to obtain Immortality
Many have been the dupe of strange drugs.
Better far to drink good wine
And clothe our bodies in robes of satin and silk.

The dead are gone and with them we cannot converse.
The living are here and ought to have our love.
Leaving the city-gate I look ahead
And see before me only mounds and tombs.
The old graves are plowed up into fields,
The pines and cypresses are hewn for timber.
In the white aspens sad winds sing;
Their long murmuring kills my heart with grief.

I want to go home, to ride to my village gate.
I want to go back, but there's no road back.

Translated from the Chinese by Arthur Waley

Thomas Mann
1875–1955

In Mann's short story "Little Herr Friedemann," the title character
has been crippled in infancy and renounces the possibility of
sensual love. This selection deals with the kind of serenity he
achieves after his mother's death and suggests how, within reduced expectations, the bereaved may still find pleasure in the
flow of daily life.

from Little Herr Friedemann

. . . in his twenty-first year his mother died, after a lingering
illness.

This was a sore blow for Johannes Friedemann, and the
pain of it endured. He cherished this grief, he gave himself up
to it as one gives oneself to a great joy, he fed it with a thousand
childhood memories; it was the first important event in his life
and he made the most of it.

Is not life in and for itself a good, regardless of whether we
may call its content "happiness"? Johannes Friedemann felt that
it was so, and he loved life. He, who had renounced the greatest
joy it can bring us, taught himself with infinite, incredible care
to take pleasure in what it had still to offer. A walk in the
springtime in the parks surrounding the town; the fragrance of
a flower; the song of a bird—might not one feel grateful for
such things as these?

And that we need to be taught how to enjoy, yes, that our education is always and only equal to our capacity for enjoyment —he knew that too, and he trained himself. Music he loved, and attended all the concerts that were given in the town. He came to play the violin not so badly himself, no matter what a figure of fun he made when he did it; and took delight in every beautiful soft tone he succeeded in producing. Also, by much reading he came in time to possess a literary taste the like of which did not exist in the place. He kept up with the new books, even the foreign ones; he knew how to savour the seductive rhythm of a lyric or the ultimate flavour of a subtly told tale—yes, one might almost call him a connoisseur.

He learned to understand that to everything belongs its own enjoyment and that it is absurd to distinguish between an experience which is "happy" and one which is not. With a right good will he accepted each emotion as it came, each mood, whether sad or gay. Even he cherished the unfulfilled desires, the longings. He loved them for their own sakes and told himself that with fulfillment the best of them would be past. The vague, sweet, painful yearning and hope of quiet spring evenings—are they not richer in joy than all the fruition the summer can bring? Yes, he was a connoisseur, our little Herr Friedemann.

But of course they did not know that, the people whom he met on the street, who bowed to him with the kindly, compassionate air he knew so well. They could not know that this unhappy cripple, strutting comically along in his light overcoat and shiny top hat—strange to say, he was a little vain—they could not know how tenderly he loved the mild flow of his life, charged with no great emotions, it is true, but full of a quiet and tranquil happiness which was his own creation. . . .

Translated from the German by H. T. Lowe-Porter

Carolyn Kizer

The Great Blue Heron

M.A.K., SEPTEMBER, 1880–SEPTEMBER, 1955

As I wandered on the beach
I saw the heron standing
Sunk in the tattered wings
He wore as a hunchback's coat.
Shadow without a shadow,
Hung on invisible wires
From the top of a canvas day,
What scissors cut him out?
Superimposed on a poster
Of summer by the strand
Of a long-decayed resort,
Poised in the dusty light
Some fifteen summers ago;
I wondered, an empty child,
"Heron, whose ghost are you?"

I stood on the beach alone,
In the sudden chill of the burned.
My thought raced up the path.
Pursuing it, I ran
To my mother in the house
And led her to the scene.
The spectral bird was gone.
But her quick eye saw him drifting
Over the highest pines
On vast, unmoving wings.
Could they be those ashen things,
So grounded, unwieldy, ragged,
A pair of broken arms
That were not made for flight?
In the middle of my loss

I realized she knew:
My mother knew what he was.

O great blue heron, now
That the summer house has burned
So many rockets ago,
So many smokes and fires
And beach-lights and water-glow
Reflecting pin-wheel and flare:
The old logs hauled away,
The pines and driftwood cleared
From that bare strip of shore
Where dozens of children play;
Now there is only you
Heavy upon my eye.
Why have you followed me here,
Heavy and far away?
You have stood there patiently
For fifteen summers and snows,
Denser than my repose,
Bleaker than any dream,
Waiting upon the day
When, like gray smoke, a vapor
Floating into the sky,
A handful of paper ashes,
My mother would drift away.

Stephen Berg

The Answer

Yes, Autumn. The leaves yellow and red.
When I got up this morning
no clouds, no thoughts, only the sky.

I slept downstairs, redreaming
the dream
where I'm talking with my father
who says he'll meet me for lunch,
his face so undeniably his that when I wake
I'm sure he will. That's why
I drove out here again. Not that he's here.
I just wanted to be by myself
with the drifting water and bright sky
so I drove fast to the spot I love between
the first stone balcony with its war heroes
and the bronze rower shipping his oars
and slid out and ran under the yellow and red trees
looking up at them as I passed and they passed.
And forgot him.
Because I can now, because
his sad, square, bitterly joking face
rises by itself through me—
the way a cloud floats in suddenly, shifts, breaks up and
        disappears—
and will until I go
back to the placelessness before us, after us.
It isn't even love that does this, or needing somebody, it isn't
even the sick miracle of being human or the leaves
blown down crackling underfoot.
I can't explain. And I'm happy not trying to.
Today your silence was what I hear every time
I go out at night
and stand still and don't look—
a chanting of stars and ants, the dry
grass and leaves congregating by accident, the buzz
of the empty world, answering.

Ruth Stone

Wild Asters

I am here to worship the blue
asters along the brook;
not to carry pollen on my legs,
Or rub strutted wings
in mindless sucking;
but to feel with my eyes
the loss of you and me,
not in the powdered mildew
that spreads from leaf to leaf,
but in the glorious absence of grief
to see what was not meant to be seen,
the clusters, the aggregate, the undenying multiplicity.

Washington Irving
1783–1859

from *The Sketch-Book*

The sorrow for the dead is the only sorrow from which we refuse
to be divorced. Every other wound we seek to heal, every other
affliction to forget; but this wound we consider it a duty to keep
open; this affliction we cherish and brood over in solitude.

Weldon Kees
1914–1955

Small Prayer

Change, move, dead clock, that this fresh day
May break with dazzling light to these sick eyes.
Burn, glare, old sun, so long unseen,
That time may find its sound again, and cleanse
Whatever it is that a wound remembers
After the healing ends.

William Shakespeare
1564–1616

from *Richard II*

You may my glories and my state depose,
But not my griefs. Still am I king of those.

May Sarton

All Souls

Did someone say that there would be an end,
An end, Oh, an end, to love and mourning?
Such voices speak when sleep and waking blend,
The cold bleak voices of the early morning
When all the birds are dumb in dark November—
Remember and forget, forget, remember.

After the false night, warm true voices, wake!
Voice of the dead that touches the cold living,
Through the pale sunlight once more gravely speak.
Tell me again, while the last leaves are falling:
"Dear child, what has been once so interwoven
Cannot be raveled, nor the gift ungiven."

Now the dead move through all of us still glowing,
Mother and child, lover and lover mated,
Are wound and bound together and enflowing.
What has been plaited cannot be unplaited—
Only the strands grow richer with each loss
And memory makes kings and queens of us.

Dark into light, light into darkness, spin.
When all the birds have flown to some real haven,
We who find shelter in the warmth within,
Listen, and feel new-cherished, new-forgiven,
As the lost human voices speak through us and blend
Our complex love, our mourning without end.

John Hall Wheelock
1886–1978

Dear Men and Women

In the quiet before cockcrow when the cricket's
Mandolin falters, when the light of the past
Falling from the high stars yet haunts the earth
And the east quickens, I think of those I love—
Dear men and women no longer with us.

And not in grief or regret merely but rather
With a love that is almost joy I think of them,

Of whom I am part, as they of me, and through whom
I am made more wholly one with the pain and the glory,
The heartbreak at the heart of things.

I have learned it from them at last, who am now grown old
A happy man, that the nature of things is tragic
And meaningful beyond words, that to have lived
Even if once only, once and no more,
Will have been—oh, how truly—worth it.

The years go by: March flows into April,
The sycamore's delicate tracery puts on
Its tender green; April is August soon;
Autumn, and the raving of insect choirs,
The thud of apples in moonlit orchards;

Till winter brings the slant, windy light again
On shining Manhattan, her towering stone and glass;
And age deepens—oh, much is taken, but one
Dearer than all remains, and life is sweet
Still, to the now enlightened spirit.

Doors are opened that never before were opened,
New ways stand open, but quietly one door
Closes, the door to the future; there it is written,
"Thus far and no farther"—there, as at Eden's gate,
The angel with the fiery sword.

The Eden we dream of, the Eden that lies before us,
The unattainable dream, soon lies behind.
Eden is always yesterday or tomorrow,
There is no way now but back, back to the past—
The past has become paradise.

And there they dwell, those ineffable presences,
Safe beyond time, rescued from death and change.

Though all be taken, they only shall not be taken—
Immortal, unaging, unaltered, faithful yet
To that lost dream world they inhabit.

Truly, to me they now may come no more,
But I to them in reverie and remembrance
Still may return, in me they still live on;
In me they shall have their being, till we together
Darken in the great memory.

Dear eyes of delight, dear youthful tresses, foreheads
Furrowed with age, dear hands of love and care—
Lying awake at dawn, I remember them,
With a love that is almost joy I remember them:
Lost, and all mine, all mine, forever.

About the Editor

MARY JANE MOFFAT received an M.A. in Creative Writing from Stanford University and taught there. She now teaches courses in writing and literature at colleges and universities in the San Francisco Bay area. With Charlotte Painter, she is coeditor of *Revelations: Diaries of Women.*